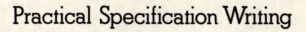

Practical Specification Writing

edited by Jack Bowyer and published by Hutchinson

Handbook of Building Crafts in Conservation

also by Jack Bowyer

Domestic Building Surveys, third edition (The Architectural Press Ltd)

Small Works Contract Documentation, third edition (The Architectural Press Ltd)

History of Building, second edition (Orion Books)

Practical Specification Writing

For architects and surveyors
Second edition

Jack Bowyer, Dipl. Arch. (Leeds), FRIBA

Hutchinson

London Melbourne Sydney Auckland Johannesburg

Hutchinson Education

An imprint of Century Hutchinson Ltd
62–65 Chandos Place, London WC2N 4NW

Century Hutchinson Australia Pty Ltd
PO Box 496, 16–22 Church Street, Hawthorn, Victoria 3122, Australia

Century Hutchinson New Zealand Ltd
PO Box 40–086, Glenfield, Auckland 10, New Zealand

Century Hutchinson South Africa (Pty) Ltd
PO Box 337, Bergvlei 2012, South Africa

First published 1981
Reprinted with amendments 1982
Second edition 1985, reprinted 1988

© Jack Bowyer, 1981, 1985

Set in IBM Journal and Pyramid

Printed and bound in Great Britain by
Anchor Brendon Ltd, Tiptree, Essex.

British Library Cataloguing in Publication Data

Bowyer, Jack
    Practical specification writing—2nd ed.
    1. Building—Contracts and specifications
    2. Specification writing
    I. Title
    692'.3   TH425

ISBN 0 09 161101 6

Contents

Acknowledgements

The author and publisher are grateful to: NBS Ltd for permission to reproduce samples of the NBS text and to NBS Services for assistance with the production of the samples; and Quentin Pickard, BA, RIBA, for reading and commenting on the early draft of the book.

Abbreviations

BS	British Standard (of the British Standard Institution)
CI/Sf.B	Construction Indexing Samarbetskommitén för Byggnadsfrågor
CP	Code of Practice (published by the British Standard Institution)
JCT	Joint Contracts Tribunal
NBS	National Building Specification
PC	Prime Cost
RIBA	Royal Institute of British Architects
SMM	Standard Method of Measurement

Introduction

Of the three documents which form the principal directives for building works – drawings, bills of quantities and specifications – only the specification has received little or no attention from revisers and has remained in essence very similar to the form in existence at the beginning of this century. Reference to F.W. Macey (*Specifications in Detail*, Spon) or J. Leaning (*Building Specifications*, Batsford) will show how little the format has changed. It is true that the text now abjures many of the detailed technical descriptions of materials and labours, replacing these with British Standard (BS) and Code of Practice (CP) references, although in many cases this has merely meant specifying down to a standard rather than up to a quality. Only recently has attention been paid in technical education to the need to develop skills in specification writing, a skill which, in all fairness is as important as draughtsmanship if the true intentions of the architect are to be fully communicated to the builder.

With reference to format, the publication of SMM6 has altered the nomenclature and grouping of many of the traditional trade sections of the bill of quantities and it appears only right that the layout and format of the specification should follow a similar pattern. The old trade barriers, in many cases, have now been abandoned on site and the grouping of clauses should follow this lead. Consequently the layouts and formats suggested in this book follow that incorporated in the latest SMM.

The object of this book is to provide the student of architecture, surveying and building with clear and concise methods for the writing of building specifications. Care is taken to relate the specification to the contract form and to show how the various types of clause may be built up to provide the necessary information required, precisely and with accuracy. As much of today's work is related to BSS and CP, a schedule of those most likely to be incorporated are included, although considerations of space preclude any details of their particular contents; consequently reference to individual publications or the official BS Handbook, which incorporates summaries of all current specifications, will be necessary in many cases.

No one type of specification can cover all the complexities of the various types of building work; alteration projects, new works, improvement grant contracts all require specifications in formats particular to each. While the basic methods of preparing and writing specific clauses are similar to all, the formats vary. In addition the preparation of draft specifications to direct the surveyor in preparing and amplifying his bill of quantities, and of specifications for the use of the specialist subcontractor or supplier in order that he may be able to interpret correctly the requirements for services and materials, are also important facets of specification writing. All are given due prominence in this book and descriptive examples are included to show and explain how each is prepared to communicate the information required.

While model clauses and standard specifications are still in use in many offices, their use must be taken as a guide and not as a formula. Each building project differs from the next and unless the description of the materials, workmanship and particular works is written with the precise requirements in mind, errors, omissions and discrepancies will occur. The publishing of the National Building Specification (NBS) has provided some material for the preparation of standard specifications and a short description of its use is included in this book (see Chapter 12).

Finally, to provide a clear and definitive text to a specification it is important to use the correct technical terminology in the relevant text. A glossary of a number of terms freely used in specification writing and the building trades, together with a concise explanation of their use and meaning, begins on page 165.

1 The purpose and use of a specification

When designer and master builder were one and the same person and the direction of building construction was an *ad hoc* affair between master and workman, the documentation involved comprised simple outline drawings and written descriptions, usually in the form of directive letters. As buildings became larger and more complicated in construction and decoration, involving the employment of numerous specialist craftsmen, the documentation of building contracts became more technical. They became even more so when the designer and builder separated into different professions, each specializing in his own particular facet of the building industry. The designer continued to direct the builder as to the form and materials to be used and the builder receiving these directions (or instructions as we now know them), built accordingly.

Two separate forms of direction or instruction have been in use in the building industry for as long as we can tell. The first and most important is the drawing which, when properly prepared to scale and annotated, indicates to the builder the overall dimensions, form or shape, fenestration and general construction of the building. Except in very small contract works, a drawing cannot incorporate all the information required by a builder to enable him to gauge the cost, particular workmanship and detail involved. He needs further direction or instruction to enable him to deal with the work, and for this he requires a document in which the designer describes or specifies his precise and particular requirements for the work in hand. This document is known as a specification, and in most building works it supplements the information incorporated in the drawings.

All building contracts require a written specification to instruct or direct for three main purposes:

1 for the use of a builder's estimator, in conjunction with the drawings, to enable him to prepare an estimate of the cost of the work prior to submitting a tender or offer;
2 for the use of the quantity surveyor, in conjunction with the drawings, to ascertain precisely the architect's intentions regarding materials and workmanship, so that he can prepare a bill of quantities, which will enable competitive tenders to be obtained for the work;
3 to be issued as an architect's instruction to the clerk of works and builder's site management staff to enable them, in conjunction with the drawings (and bill of quantities if prepared), to interpret the architect's precise intentions in respect of materials to be used and standard of workmanship to be employed.

In addition to the full written specification, short specifications are often required to cover portions of the work, specific materials or items forming a portion of the whole contract. Examples of these are:

(a) specifications for electrical or heating installations to enable an estimate to be obtained against a Prime Cost Sum included in the original contract

(b) specifications for specialist building work, such as underpinning a foundation, or for specific items of joinery or fittings when details of the requirements were not available at the time the main specification was written, covering the work either by a Provisional or a Prime Cost Sum.

These latter specifications omit much of the full specification and include only such information as is specific to the particular work to be described.

Where the specification is used as a basis (with the drawings) for the preparation of a tender, the value of the work will generally be either small or the works relatively simple in format. A housing contract involving the erection of a small number of identical units, the conversion of a property into a number of flats or a small warehouse or factory project, for example, generally use the specification as a basis for estimating and contract. In these instances, the builder's estimator prepares his own 'builder's quantities' from the information shown on the drawings and included in the specification document. He will only measure and price such materials, workmanship and items included; any omissions will be excluded from the contract and will form the subject of extras if required, the builder being entitled to extra payment for the work. It therefore follows that the specification must not only be complete, to avoid undesirable extras, but also clear in intention so that the estimator can be in no doubt as to the architect's requirements.

The specification prepared originally for the instruction of the quantity surveyor must also be as complete and precise as that supplied for the use of the builder. However, initially it can be issued as a handwritten document, with any amendments found necessary during the preparation of the bill of quantities being added in red ink before the document is typed for issuing to the site. The quantity surveyor will use this specification (in conjunction with the drawings) to prepare his descriptions and write his bill for the work. While omissions in the original text can be picked up and added at this stage, care must be taken to ensure that the specification, when typed, relates precisely to the descriptions incorporated in the bill of quantities.

When work on the contract commences on site, the site supervisory staff, acting for both architect and client, and the contractor will require copies of the specification

(a) to keep them informed of the basis on which the builder's estimator priced the work where drawings and specification only form the basis of tender and contract, *or*

(b) to indicate to them the basis on which the quantity surveyor prepared his measured bill of quantities with its descriptions of materials and particular workmanship.

In the first case, the full specification should provide virtually the complete information necessary to supplement and embellish the drawings; the only additional instruction needed would be in respect of the expenditure of Prime Cost and Provisional Sums. In the second case, the specification should supplement information contained in the bill of quantities and should be restricted to information that would affect the price, for example, the precise location of items is dealt with in the specification such as the positioning of fittings in a certain room. Instructions regarding the spacing of timbers are also of importance to the pratical construction of the building, but are irrelevant to the quantities where volumetric considerations are paramount. It can be seen, therefore, that the specification which supplements a bill of quantities is a different document from a full specification and should be prepared with the contents of the bill in mind in order to prevent repetition.

The writing of specifications requires great powers of concentration and a full and detailed knowledge of building materials, methods of working and craftsmanship. Too many specifications are badly written, slipshod and inprecise and can open the way to claims for extras. A specification writer must be

(a)   clear as to exactly what the architect has in mind when he prepared or issued the detail drawings for the project;

(b)   able to express the architect's requirements in clear, technical and precise written form free from any ambiguity.

Unless the designer knows what he wants he cannot expect either the specification writer to describe it, the estimator to price it or the builder to construct it. It is the duty of the specification writer to either extract the information or to deal with the work by means of a specific sum to be included in the contract and expended on the work when details are finalized. The writing of the specification must be in clear, simple English, avoiding unnecessarily long or complicated words, and using technical words in their true and proper context.

Finally, the descriptions of work included in a specification must be practical and capable of being constructed. Materials must be used where they are capable of proper performance and their fixing must be in accordance with proper trade practice. Qualities of materials and workmanship should be not only reasonably obtainable but should also be appropriate to the particular project contemplated. Care must also be taken to specify bearing in mind the requirements of statutory instruments as well as the limitations of both the material suppliers and the transport and site handlers; and always to specify up to a standard rather than down to a regulation.

2 The preparation of a specification

Before starting to write a specification, the writer must be in possession of all the information necessary for the work and must also decide the form it is to take.

The information necessary generally comprises a full set of drawings, including such details as are necessary to amplify and explain the layout drawings, together with such schedules as are required for the project. The schedules should include:

internal finishes
doors and windows incorporating ironmongery
joinery fittings
sanitary fittings
Prime Cost and Provisional Sums

The drawings should incorporate, in addition to full material annotation:

serial numbers to all doors and windows
room titles or numbers
full details of external material finishes indicated on the elevation
full details of construction at changes of material or construction techniques
all drainage runs, manholes and special fittings
location of pipe runs and services
location of all joinery and sanitary fittings

All this information will be required by the contractor during the progress of the work and is essential for the specification writer if he is to carry out his work in a proper manner.

The form of the specification will depend largely on the type of building work to be described, the form of contract to be used or the method by which the work is to be financed. The main forms of specification employed can be described as follows:

(a) Specifications for new buildings, generally written in trade form, in which the work is traditionally broken down and described in sections relating to individual building trades – for example, Excavation and earthwork, Concrete work, Brickwork and blockwork, etc. This is the traditional form of building specification, well understood by both quantity surveyors and builders. Quantity surveyors prefer to use this form as an instruction for quantities as in general it follows the form generally adopted in preparing surveyors' bills of quantities (see Chapter 9). This traditional form has been amended in SMM6 but the general format is still retained.

(b)   Specifications for alteration works in which it is convenient for the bulk of the work to be described in sequence room by room. Works of demolition, repairs or alterations to the external fabric, electrical and plumbing service installations and external works can be specified separately as required. It is also convenient to incorporate at the beginning of the specification a separate section describing in general terms the materials and standards of workmanship required, as this will considerably reduce repetition in the separate works descriptions. The work in individual rooms may best be described as a series of spot items, each concerned solely with a single item of work, for example:

The removal of a door and frame and the blocking of the opening
Formation of a new partition and its finishing
The precise decoration of a wall or room

(c)   Specifications for work which is to be the subject of an application for a statutory financial grant. In this type of specification, which in general follows that of the specification for alteration works, the works to be carried out as 'improvements' must be kept financially separate from other works such as 'repairs'. The specification must indicate which items of work refer to improvement or repair, and allow the builder's estimator to give a separate price for each item. (See Chapter 10.) The specification includes cash and collection columns on each page for this, a full collection sheet being provided at the end so that the subtotals can be collected for transfer to the form of tender (see Chapter 11).

Once the necessary information has been provided and the form of specification has been decided upon, the text can be prepared. The point has already been made that the specification must be written in clear, simple English, avoiding unnecessarily long or complicated words. It is essentially a document for quick reference and comprehension, ideally divided into short paragraphs under clear headings for the benefit of the builder. Information should be precise and definite; where alternatives are acceptable, they should be clearly indicated, and the contractor made aware of them without any confusion. Sentences should be short and punctuation direct.

All descriptions should be consistent in content. Words or phrases used should not be used in different senses in different parts of the text or confusion and perhaps disputes may occur. Dimensions should be given in the accepted order — length: width (or depth): height — varying only for steel joists and steel windows, which are given as height x width. Timber may be described as 'finished', 'prepared' or 'wrot' to indicate a planed surface. The description selected is immaterial so long as the word used to describe the surface is used consistently throughout. Nominal sizes should be used to describe timber which is to be planed, the allowance for working to conform to the relevant British Standard (BS 4471, Pt 1: 1978).

Specifications must be drafted in a suitable form for typing. It is practically impossible to dictate a specification as, in most cases, the writer will need to return to his text on numerous occasions to insert, remove or alter material. A written draft is usual, the writing confined to alternate lines with space left for insertions and alterations. Each trade or section of the specification should commence on a separate sheet of paper, with each trade or section written out in full, in the sequences given in the examples (see page 55). Only one side of the paper should be written on, the backs used for insertions as necessary, preferably in red ink to assist the typist. In most specifications the clauses describing the bulk of the building work will be written first; the preliminaries, materials and workmanship clauses and schedules are usually written at the end and then inserted in the correct position in the draft.

Quick reference is a vital feature of any specification and is obtained by clear numbering of individual clauses. This enables cross-references to be written throughout the text and also allows quick reference from the table of contents or index, if provided. Numbering of clauses should be deferred until the whole specification has been completed. Two methods are in common use. In the first, each clause throughout the text is numbered, ignoring any break for change of trade or section, and giving a continuous sequence of numbers from first clause to last, for example:

126   Provide double course of tiles at eaves.

This method is ideal but, as so often happens, problems can arise when an omission occurs and a clause has to be inserted under an alphabetical suffix.

The second method, which is now in more common use, incorporates a principal numbering system for each trade or section followed by duo-decimal numbering for each separate clause, for example:

9.03   Provide double course of tiles at eaves.

This enables clauses to be added at the end of each trade section without disturbing the numbering of following clauses and appears to be a neater alternative. Whichever method is used, it is best to place the numbering at the left-hand margin and to follow it with the clause heading, if provided.

Underlining, as a means of drawing attention to salient matters should be restricted to those which are actually important. Trade or section headings, Prime Cost and Provisional Sums, omissions and credits are the only items which should be accentuated by underlining:

9.06   **Vertical tiling. Cover the cheeks of dormers with approved sand-faced hand-made clay plain tiles, etc.**

12.19   **Sanitary fittings. Include the PC Sum of £350.00 for the supply and delivery to site, etc.**

2.24   **Contingencies. Include the Provisional Sum of £750.00 for contingencies, the sum to be expended, etc.**

Statutory controls and instruments are of great importance and must be carefully borne in mind during the writing of a specification. A great deal of control over both workmanship and materials used in building is provided by the Building Regulations (and their 'deemed to satisfy' provisions, including British Standards and Codes of Practice), the London Building Acts and the Scottish Building Regulations. The responsibility for describing methods of construction and materials that comply with these regulations falls directly on the architect (as designer) and the specification writer. The builder's obligations in this respect are limited to carrying out the works in a proper and workmanlike manner, which includes preparing the works, notifying the Building Control Staff as required and attending on and assisting them with equipment or staff when carrying out statutory inspections or testing. It is therefore essential that the specification writer is fully aware of the provisions and limitations of the 'deemed to satisfy' requirements of building legislation and that he writes his specification with this fully in mind.

In some contracts, the building owner will wish, or will be in a position, to supply particular equipment or materials for use in the works. He may wish, for example, to remove a water softener from his present house and to incorporate it in a new house, or he may be able to supply stone, timber, bricks or fittings from his own business. There is nothing in either of the contracts in general use to prohibit this, but the contractor must be fully aware of what is involved and what attendance or duties will fall on him in the matter, for which he must make financial provision in his estimate. The matter may be dealt with by the inclusion in the specification of a provisional sum (see Chapter 3). Ideally, if the information can be obtained, a specification clause should be written and inserted in the appropriate trade or work section to enable the estimator to price the work, for example:

10.32 <u>Fitted wardrobe</u>. The contractor is to include in his estimate for carefully removing a fitted wardrobe situated in a first floor bedroom at No. 13, Carlisle Road, Swinton, covering up and protecting same, transporting to site, offloading, moving to position and refixing in position indicated on the drawings. Include for making all arrangements for access, providing all skilled workmen required, transport and protection.

It will be seen here that the fitting has to be removed, transported and refixed. In some instances the item may be of a simpler nature, for example:

9.01 <u>Roofing tiles</u>. The roofing tiles will be 265 x 165 mm second-hand antique sand-faced plain tiles supplied to site by the employer at no cost to the contractor. Include for offloading and stacking tiles in position adjacent to hardstanding.

The builder here is supplied with material at no cost but has to offload and stack it for use in the works. The actual fixing of the tiles would be described in later clauses in the specification.

A table of contents is essential to any specification. Good indexes can be valuable, but they are time-consuming to prepare and, unless they are accurate and comprehensive, they are liable to be ignored.

Reproduction from a typed copy can be carried out by a number of methods, all of which, so long as the original is clear, provide satisfactory copies. Before reproduction, the proof must be read with care and any errors corrected. Sufficient copies should be taken off to suit the work involved and the contract requirements.

3 The specification and the form of contract

Where bills of quantities are not required for a building project it will follow that the specification becomes a vital part of the contract. Where quantities form part of the contract, the specification is of an explanatory or directive nature only. This has been fully described in Chapter 1.

Three documents are in general use for building contracts where the specification is the descriptive and explanatory basis for the contract works.

The *Standard Form* of building contract, for use without quantities, is published for the Joint Contracts Tribunal by RIBA Publications Ltd in two variants:

(a) as a local authority's edition in general use for all public works except those under the direction of the Property Services Agency of the Department of the Environment, and

(b) the private edition which is in general use for all building projects carried out in private sector construction work.

The *Intermediate Form of Contract* is published for the Joint Contracts Tribunal and in its standard form can be used for contracts, with or without quantities, for both private and local authority contracts. Its use is primarily for medium-size contracts where subcontracts are of a simple uncomplicated nature.

The *Agreement for Minor Building Works* is also published for the Joint Contracts Tribunal by RIBA Publications Ltd but is not issued for use in Scotland.

The Standard Form of contract is a larger and more complex document than the two other forms of contract and its requirements in respect of the specification are greater than those for the simpler contract form. The reason for this is that works carried out under the Standard Form are generally more complex and involve greater sums of money, the problems of contract management are more complicated, and the areas of dispute or disagreement are wider and need a legalistic approach for their solution. The Standard Form, however, contains certain features, namely Prime Cost Sums and Provisional Sums, the latter being also included in the IFC contract, where the name of the proposed subcontractor must be added.

Prime Cost (PC) Sums
However carefully an architect may carry out his preparatory work, and however willing an employer may be to agree all matters pertaining to the contract works before tenders are invited, there are always areas of work or materials to be supplied which are either outside a builder's normal work or where final selection cannot be made until the actual building works are reasonably advanced. Examples of such matters are specialist work normally carried out by subcontractors, for example structural steelwork, precast

concrete floors, electrical installations, etc., or materials which, while basically similar, are subject to infinite variation in construction, colour or finish, for example sanitary fittings, ironmongery or wallpapers.

Where the work is of a specialist nature outside the builder's general experience it is usual for the architect to nominate a firm of specialists to do the work. If the builder accepts the nomination, he will let the work to the specialists, who become nominated subcontractors for the work as specified. To enable a builder to include a sum in his estimate for the work and to put all builders tendering on the same basis, a clause is incorporated in the specification to cover the inclusion of a sum of money, known as a Prime Cost Sum (PC Sum), to cover the cost of a specified item of work. For example:

14.01   <u>Structural steelwork. Include the Prime Cost Sum of £7750.00</u> for the fabrication, delivery to site and erection complete of the structural steel frame, the work to be carried out by a specialist contractor to be nominated by the architect.

The contractor's estimator will therefore include the sum of £7750.00 in his estimate but unless he is instructed further he will leave this sum as net, making no allowance for any other costs or profit involved. The specification must therefore include further directions so that the builder, when making up his estimate, will include all the extra costs involved in the specialist's work; this prevents the builder from coming back to the architect later in the contract for extras:

Add for all necessary attendance and profit.

The addition of this sentence instructs the builder to include for all extra assistance the steelwork erectors will normally require in carrying out their work, for example access on to the site for their crane, hardstanding for the crane in operation, space for the steelwork to be offloaded and sorted, power and light if required, the use of water and sanitary conveniences, etc. He will also include in his estimate for his profit as an addition to the PC Sum.

There are, however, other matters which must be covered relating to trades or specialist items and these are described later in the specific sections. The PC Sum included in the specification is used as a basis for competitive tendering and can be altered by architect's instruction or variation order after the contract is let, either by increasing or decreasing the sum as applicable. In any event the sum incorporated in the specification will be subject to adjustment against the specialist's account when the final account is prepared.

A second use for Prime Cost Sums is for the supply of materials or equipment which the builder, within his general sphere of work, would be competent to fix; for such work the builder would also employ staff in the various trades, for example, to install and fix sanitary fittings; to hang iron gates; to install solid fuel stoves and boilers. The materials themselves, being produced in a wide variety of designs, shapes, finishes and perhaps sizes, or specially designed by the architect to meet the employer's particular fancy, would be supplied by a specialist merchant or made in a specialist craft workshop and delivered to site, the cost again being covered by the inclusion of a Prime Cost Sum in the relevant trade section of the specification by the architect.

12.19   <u>Sanitary fittings.</u> Include the Prime Cost Sum of £650.00 for the supply and delivery to site of sanitary fittings by a merchant to be nominated by the architect.

The supplier here becomes a nominated supplier under the terms of the contract and the builder includes the specified sum in his estimate. Again, he has other expenses in this matter which must be covered and his profit must be added. Therefore a further direction is added to remove any possibility of a claim for an extra.

Add for profit, taking delivery, storing as required, moving to position, assembling and fixing complete the following items of sanitary ware:

Here follows a schedule of the items included in the quotation and basic directions for the builder to fix as follows:

1 no. 1700 mm coloured porcelain enamelled cast-iron bath complete with side panel, shower unit, overflow, waste, plug and chain, and wall-mounted pivoted glass shower screen.
2 no. coloured vitreous china low level coupled syphonic WC suites complete with plastic seat and cover.
2 no. 700 x 500 mm coloured vitreous china pedestal wash basins complete with 900 x 500 mm mirror splashback, taps, outlet, plug and chain.

The Prime Cost Sums included for the supply of materials or equipment are, of course (subject to the terms of the contract) adjusted by the suppliers account in the preparation of the final account for the building contract.

Provisional Sums

Circumstances occur in the preparation of a specification where a close and specific description of an item or artefact is not possible owing to lack of information. For example, in an alteration contract the precise nature of the existing structure may not be known, or the depth or position of a particular drain or service may not be precisely indicated. To cover such eventualities and the work likely in connection with the architect's intentions, a sum is included which is known to be subject to adjustment when the full nature of the work can be gauged or ascertained. This is known as a Provisional Sum. These sums are calculated to include the cost of the work, profit and attendance; the actual cost of the work is often calculated on a daywork basis. For example:

7.24   Include the Provisional Sum of £250.00 for opening up the brick wall over the main entrance porch, repairing or replacing the defective lead tray and making good all work disturbed.

Another use for Provisional Sums is to cover the cost of work carried out by local authorities (for example, pavement crossings) and stautory undertakers (for example, gas, water and electricity services). The actual cost of the work carried out will eventually be charged to the builder and the sum included must be sufficient to cover both this account and the builder's overheads, attendance and profit. For example:

12.14   Include the Provisional Sum of £150.00 for a 15 mm main water service to the building.

Care must be taken to specify exactly the amount of work covered by the Provisional Sum and how much additional work is to be included for in the builder's estimate. For example, gas board services and electricity supplies terminate within a building, and their cost includes connection to and supply of a suitable meter. Water supply authorities, on the other hand, terminate their services at a stopcock or meter situated on the boundary of the site, so the builder must be instructed to extend them to a position within the building with the necessary control.

19.15   Excavate for new main water service to a depth not less than 750 mm below the finished ground level from the water authority's service to the stopcock position within the building. Supply and run a 15 mm copper service pipe wrapped in Denso tape terminating in a brass screw-down combined stop and drain cock to BS 1010, Pt 2: 1973. Carefully return, fill in over and consolidate excavated material over new service pipe and make good any work disturbed.

As payment for these services by the authorities concerned are strictly net and do not allow for a cash discount, the builder must be instructed to add to his estimate to cover the 2½ per cent discount loss.

Add 2½% to the value of the Provisional Sum to cover for loss of discount.

As all building contracts require a 'float' to cover unforeseen eventualities it is usual to include a sum of money in the contract to provide for such contingencies. For example, a strata of unconsolidated subsoil may be discovered under a foundation necessitating extra excavation and foundation works. Unless provision has been made in the specification for such an unforeseen occurrence, delay might cause a partial closing down of the works while authority for extra work is obtained and the necessary funds provided to cover the cost. It is usual to include, as a Provisional Sum, a sum of money in the specification for contingencies, inclusive of profit and any attendance, to be expended in accordance with the architect's instructions.

2.24   Contingencies. Include the Provisional Sum of £750.00 for contingencies, to be used as directed by the architect and deducted in whole or part if not required.

The sum included is generally 5 per cent of the estimated value of new works, and 10 to 15 per cent on alteration works.

The inclusion, therefore, of Prime Cost and Provisional Sums in the specification covers situations which, however carefully the project is thought out and detailed, will occur in practice and for which both the contract forms in common use make provision.

   A final requirement of a specification is that it informs the estimator of the specific inclusions which will be incorporated in the main text or in the Appendix at the end of the selected form of contract. There are a number of clauses in these contracts of which the period of time, percentage of cost or monetary value is subject to the precise requirements of the building owner or to the discretion of the architect. As these will considerably affect the total estimate or offer of the builder it is necessary that he should be in full possession of the information when he is preparing his estimate. In the Agreement for Minor Building Works there is no separate Appendix but there are clauses which require insertions or deletion of alternatives; some of these will affect the value of the estimate. A separate section of the specification should therefore be devoted to describing the contract to be used; it should list any alterations to the standard text as well as inclusions that will be enforced in the contract and for which the contractor must make monetary provision in his estimate. The layout of this and suggested clauses are described in Chapter 7.

4 Building up material and workmanship clauses

In the main body of the specification dealing specifically with the works to be carried out, as opposed to the administrative details of contracts and preliminary items, the clauses fall quite clearly into two separate divisions: materials and workmanship, and specific work clauses. These clauses must convey to the estimator and the builder exactly the *quality* of the work required. The drawings convey overall dimensions, spatial content and juxtaposition of building elements but generally little else. The specification conveys detail, both as to the quality of the workmanship to be employed and the materials to be used, as well as describing the methods to be employed in the construction. Specific work clauses and methods for their construction are described in Chapter 5.

The writing of descriptive clauses to convey the precise requirements of workmanship is a most exacting task. At one time it was possible to convey this information to competent builders simply by describing the type of building under construction or by indicating in the preliminaries a model to emulate. This is no longer possible as standards, in most building work today, are low. Another method was to describe the work as 'of the best quality', but again this is not possible as the terms 'best' and 'quality' are open now to very wide interpretation. Today, the general method of defining a standard of quality is either to exhaustively describe the work; or to employ only contractors whose standards suit precisely the work in hand and who can be relied upon to carry out the work to this agreed standard; or, as in most specifications today, to use the standards of quality laid down in either specific BS Codes of Practice or by recognized specialist craft associations and to incorporate the relevant references or clauses in the specification.

The Codes of Practice dealing with the quality of workmanship in the building industry are numerous and cover most of the trades employed. A schedule incorporating the principal British Standard Specifications and Codes of Practice applicable to the building industry is given in Chapter 6.

Alteration works Specifications for alteration works generally deal with specific work items on a room-to-room basis, presenting these as spot items. It will be obvious that such a specification will become too lengthy unless the specific requirements in respect of materials and workmanship are collected together in one section. This is then the method used for this type of work, the later work clauses being deemed to imply acceptance of the standards of quality previously described.

It will be apparent that material and workmanship clauses cannot be drafted before the work clauses are prepared, with the exception of relatively standardized works that are simple to execute. Standard descriptions, such as for Concrete work in respect of the qualities of aggregates, cement and mixes to be employed, and Brickwork and Blockwork in respect of bonding, labours and mortars, can of course be prepared, but with Woodwork, Plumbing and Mechanical Engineering Services and Painting and Decorating, the use of a standard description could lead to errors and omissions. It is therefore more satisfactory to prepare material and workmanship clauses after the work clauses have been completed and checked.

Material and workmanship clauses in alteration work specifications should form the second part of the document, following immediately after the preliminaries and general conditions and before the specific work clauses. The layout can generally follow that for a new works specification with the various trade sections listed in order generally accepted by the building industry:

General specification of materials and workmanship

Demolition
Excavation and earthworks
Concrete work
Brickwork and blockwork
Rubble walling and masonry
Asphalt work
Roofing
Woodwork
Structural steelwork
Metalwork
Plumbing and mechanical engineering services
Electrical installations
Floor, wall and ceiling finishes
Glazing
Painting and decorating
Drainage
Fencing

As most trade sections will contain a limited number of separate clauses, all clauses can be numbered consecutively, the trades being indicated simply by an underlined heading.

3.52　All glass is to be left clean and polished both sides. Any cracked or broken panes are to be hacked out and renewed and the whole left clean and perfect on completion.

3.53　Painting and decorating. Paints and emulsions generally will be manufactured by . . . and used strictly in accordance with their recommendations.

3.54　No external painting will be carried out in wet, foggy or frosty weather or when surfaces are not properly dry, and internally before the premises are rendered free from dust, etc.

The clauses describing the quality of materials are prepared differently according to the method of description used.

Example A

3.17   <u>Bricks</u>. The external facings for the works will be 65mm approved first hard multi-stock facings to match existing equal to a sample to be approved in bulk by the architect.

Here the onus is on the contractor to assess the quality of the existing work and to arrange for both a price (to enable him to build up a rate for his tender) and samples for the approval of the architect. He has, in fact, to shop around for both quality and price.
A second method could be specified as follows:

3.17   <u>Bricks</u>. Include the PC Sum of £160.00 per thousand for 65 mm stock facing bricks to be supplied and delivered to site by a manufacturer to be nominated by the architect.

Here the supply of bricks is dealt with as a Prime Cost item for delivery under nomination, the architect taking it upon himself to shop around and select the bricks he requires for the job.
A third method of specifying is as follows:

3.17   <u>Bricks</u>. The external facings for the works will be 65mm approved first hard multi-stock facings to be supplied by . . . and equal to a sample approved by the architect.

Here the brick is described by the manufacturer's stock description and the contractor is left to make his own arrangements as to price. However, in all cases a short description as to the standard of quality required for the delivered bricks should be added.

3.18   **The facing bricks shall be sound, hard, well burnt, truly shaped, free from all defects and inclusions.**

This description sets the standards required for the material as delivered to site.

Example B

3.17   Bricks. The bricks for foundation work will be approved Class B clay bricks conforming to BS 3921: 1974.

The British Standard quoted lays down certain requirements and standards for both foundation, facing and common bricks and while these may be quite satisfactory for the class of work for which they are required, they might not be satisfactory for good class alterations and extension work.
The examples given above can be used as a basis for preparing clauses on most building materials, with adjustments for the particular requirements and features of, for example, building blocks, aggregates, windows, doors, tiles and slates, glass, paint, etc.
Qualities of workmanship can be described by a similar method, but in general, more detail for specific trades is required. Where possible it is better to describe the workmanship precisely than to use a Code of Practice description. For example, in Brickwork and blockwork:

3.21   Mortar below d.p.c. and above roof level will be 1:3 cement and sand; otherwise mortar will be compo 1:1:6.

3.22   Four courses of brickwork will rise 300 mm and pointing will be carried out as the work proceeds with the joint cut off flush with the trowel and the whole lightly brushed to remove surface laitence.

There are, however, trades where workmanship can be more easily related to a Code of Practice, for example, Asphalt work (CP 144, Pt 4: 1970); Sanitary pipework (BS 5572: 1978).

A typical clause drafted to incorporate the specific requirements of a Code of Practice might be as follows:

3.38   Plastering. The internal plastering shall be carried out strictly in accordance with the requirements of BS 5492: 1977.

Alternatively in small works alterations, the specification might well read:

3.38   Workmanship. All walls and ceilings shall be finished straight and smooth. All cracks, blemishes, blows and rough areas are to be cut out and made good on completion.

New works   The layout of a specification for new works varies from that prepared for alterations in that is broken up into separate trade sections (as listed on page 22) with the addition of the Preliminary and general contract clauses which, as in all specifications, are placed at the beginning of the document. Each trade section incorporates both material and workmanship clauses and specific work clauses, the latter following on.

14.00   Glazing

14.01   Materials. All glass is to be ordinary glazing quality complying with the requirements of BS 952, Pt 1: 1978. Putty is to be linseed oil to BS 544: 1969 for glazing to wood and approved best quality metal-glazing compound for glazing to metal.

14.02   Workmanship. All rebates are to have one coat of appropriate primer paint applied prior to the commencement of glazing. All glass is to be cut to fit easily into the rebates, sprigged or clipped and back puttied and puttied the full depth of the rebate or sight lines and neatly cleaned off on completion.

14.03   Sheet glass. Glass generally is to be 4 mm clear sheet unless specified to the contrary.

14.04   Obscured glass. Glaze the following in Group 2 obscured glass to selected patterns:
Doors: D2, D6 and D8
Windows: W5, W6 and W12

14.05   All glass is to be left clean and polished both sides. Any cracked or broken panes are to be hacked out and renewed and the whole of the glazing left clean and perfect on completion.

The sequence in each trade section, then, is to specify the materials, workmanship and work, with a final clause to cover accidental damage and its repair or replacement within both the period and the terms of the contract. This format is used for the bulk of specifications dealing with new works and is applicable to all trades.

5 Building up work clauses

Work clauses are primarily descriptions of work to be carried out, whereas precise material specifications describe, as we saw in Chapter 4, the exact physical standards required for the various materials that will be incorporated in the contract works. This definition does not, however, totally exclude the descriptions in work clauses of materials to be used in specific works. The selection of grades or strengths of material are often to be found in work clauses, and the principal description or specifications of the work given at length in material clauses. For example, for concrete, the specification clause describing selection of aggregates, proportion of mixes, integration, transportation and placing would be located in the material clauses section, and the specified mix of concrete in a particular situation would be given in the work clauses section of the specification. Other examples come readily to mind, for example, the precise description of blocks and their BS references given in the material clauses and their location in specific situations in the work clauses.

Alteration works The preparation of a series of specification clauses to describe a particular work situation must follow a sequence which is both logical and unambiguous. The best method is to set out the work clauses in the sequence in which the builder would carry out the work. This method has a number of advantages:

(a) There is less likelihood of omission.
(b) The estimator can follow the sequence of work clearly and logically, which is a great help in building up an estimate for the work.
(c) The builder can carry out the work in sequence, following the directions incorporated in the clauses, and will be less likely to misinterpret the architect's intentions.

Before commencing to draft the clauses a list of work units should be compiled, each dealing with an individual action necessary to carry out the work, the whole forming a continuous work-flow extending possibly over a number of trades to complete the work unit. Take the example of forming an opening in an existing wall and inserting a new door and lining to suit. The list of work units would run as follows:

Needle, prop and strut (temporary support)
Break through existing wall
Cut away for, provide, hoist and bed new lintel and pin up over
Remove existing skirting and set aside for re-use

Cut away and form new opening
Prepare and make good to reveals
Provide and insert new lining
Make out floor through opening
Make good to plaster
Provide and fix new architrave
Cut, fit and replace skirting
Provide and hang new door on butt hinges as specified
Provide and fit lock and door furniture
Decorate and make out decorations to walls, etc.

Two other items will be applicable:
Clear away debris
Clean floors, etc.

but these will usually be covered by general clauses in the Preliminaries and can be ignored here. In addition, if the opening is to an external wall a work unit for enclosing and protecting the opening against intrusion and weather may be added at the beginning of the work description; again, however, in most cases a general clause dealing with protection may well be included in the Preliminaries.

Having prepared a logical sequence of work units to complete the whole, and possessing (a) the details of construction and finishing of the existing structure as a result of a site inspection, and (b) the architect's requirements in respect of joinery, ironmongery and decorative finishes, etc., the specification writer can write the work clauses for this item.

5.23   **New door D27.** Needle, prop and strut as required, break through existing half brick wall, cut away for, form new 150 x 100 mm concrete (mix C) lintel with 150 mm bearing at each end and reinforced with 1 no. 12 mm m.s. bar, hoist and bed in position and pin up over in stout slates in cement mortar.

As the practical constructor, the builder is liable for the safety and stability of the building; none the less, his attention should be drawn to his obligations. For example, the thickness of the wall should be stated, as should the dimensions and bearing of the lintel; the lintel's length, however, will vary depending on the 'building-in tolerance' the builder will allow on site between the new reveal and the back of the frame. The concrete mix will have been described in the material clauses as will the end preparation of the steel bars. The space between the top of the lintel and the opening must be securely and solidly filled, the proportion of the mortar mix being again specified in the material clauses.

5.24   Remove existing skirting (both sides) and carefully set aside on site for re-use. Cut away existing brickwork to suit new door and lining, prepare and form new reveals, all properly bonded to existing work.

At this point the builder would remove any temporary supports but no direction should be given to him to do so for the reasons given before.

5.25   Provide a new 38 mm wrot, rebated and rounded softwood lining tongued together at the corners, bedding face primed, securely fixed with long stout sheradized screws with pelleted heads to hardwood pellets, 3 no. to each reveal.

The width of the lining is not specified as this will depend on the exact overall wall thickness; while 12 mm or so either way will make little difference to the estimate as it is prepared, over- or under-sized linings are expensive to alter after manufacture. In principle, if a width is specified the builder will work to this; if not, he will have to measure for it accurately as required. The priming may have been included in the general material descriptions but the method of fixing to reveals should be specified: hardwood pallets built into the bedding joints of the reveals to take sheradized countersunk fixing screws with pelleted heads (or cut nails with stopped heads) are generally used to fix new frames to openings formed on old walls; sheradized fixing cramps are used in new work where the lining or frame is stood up and the walls built to them.

5.26   Make out softwood boarded floor through opening, all to match existing with ends of boards carried on softwood bearers and all securely cramped up and nailed down.

5.27   Cut back existing plaster to sound as required, level up work and make good all disturbed in two-coat work, all to match existing.

Cutting away for the opening can loosen old plaster and this must be removed before any making good is carried out. The mix is not important but the new should match the existing. If the existing is not satisfactory or loose the whole wall plaster should be hacked off and all renewed.

5.28   Provide and fix to both sides of lining 75 × 19 mm moulded softwood architrave to detail, properly and neatly mitred at the angles. Bedding face to be primed before fixing.

If the architrave is a BS stock pattern the appropriate reference would be indicated instead. External angles are always mitred but in good class work a plinth block would be specified and the architrave described as 'cut and fitted' to same.

5.29   Take from store, cut, fit, prime bedding surfaces and re-fix existing skirting to both sides of new opening.

5.30   Provide and hang to new lining on 1½ pairs of 75 mm pressed steel butts, 1 no. 35 mm thick, 762 × 1829 mm internal flush door to BS 459, Pt 2: 1962.

Except for very light construction flush doors which can be hung on a single pair of butt hinges, doors should be hung on one and a half pairs to spread the weight of the door more evenly over the height of the frame, to resist movement in the door and to reduce sheer on the screws. This is especially important where thin linings are employed as here only short screws with little purchase can be used. The precise specification for the door or reference to detail drawings should be incorporated in the description.

5.31   Provide and fix to door 1 no. 2 lever upright mortise lock with steel case and brass forend and keep PC £2.50, with 1 no. set SAA lever handles with long backplate PC £2.75 per set. Fix items with matching screws, lightly oil lock and ease and adjust as necessary on completion.

Ironmongery can be specified as above, where the estimator includes the sums in his estimate, or incorporated in a PC Sum to cover the whole of the material and included in the material clauses. With a small quantity of ironmongery it is perhaps simpler to specify as above. In any event the last sentence is important as it covers both quality of fixing and extra items so often necessary, usually forgotten and ultimately appearing as an extra in final accounts.

5.32   Prepare, knot, prime with wood primer as specified, stop and paint all new woodwork one undercoat and one coat gloss finish. Prepare, wash off and rub down existing painted skirting, stop, touch up bare wood with primer, bring forward as necessary and paint one undercoat and one coat gloss finish. Wash off and rub down existing emulsioned wall surface, prepare new plaster, cutting out and filling in all cracks and blow holes and rubbing down as necessary. Apply one mist coat to new plaster followed by two full coats emulsion on whole wall face.

Specification clauses for decoration must always be precise and clear as the labour content in this trade forms the bulk of the costs. Priming bedding surfaces will have been included in each work clause, but where the surface is exposed the application of shellac knotting to resinous areas of the timber and exposed knots is necessary to prevent bleeding through the paint film; in addition, holes and uneven patches need filling and levelling up. The minimum paint specification for wood surfaces is two coats, extra undercoats being specified in better class work.

Repainting existing painted work requires washing off and rubbing down the existing gloss finish to provide adhesion for the new paint film, as well as removing dirt and other substances on the surface that would interfere with the new paint system. Where required, the whole of the paint system should be burnt off and the whole process commenced again. Bare wood needs touching up with primer, and depressions filled in (or brought forward) to provide a flat, even finished surface to the paintwork.

Existing painted wall surfaces also need washing off and rubbing down for similar reasons. New plaster usually shrinks away from old and pin-holes and similar defects need filling in and rubbing down before paint is applied. A thin or mist coat of emulsion is best applied to new plaster to reduce suction on the full coats.

From the example given, covering work in a number of trades, it will be seen how work clauses are built up to describe in logical sequence a particular item of building work. These may include forming an opening in a roof or floor, the insertion of a window or ventilator, the removal of a chimney stack or fireplace. The method for each is identical and so long as the strict sequence of work is followed and described in logical order a clear and precise specification will follow.

New works

Writing work clauses for specifications covering new work is much simpler than for alteration works. The basic rules still apply and the various clauses should continue to follow the sequence in which the work is carried out. For example, in roof tiling the sequence of operations is:

General roof slopes

Eaves
Verges and abutments
Hips and valleys

By incorporating within these clauses the particular requirements of the work the specification follows the logical course of the tiling. The specification ends with the Completion clause, which covers replacement of chipped or broken tiles, defects in pointing, clearing out gutters, etc., and directions to leave the roofs perfect and weathertight.

With single work clauses specifying complete items, a slightly different method may be used. For example, timber floor specifications in woodwork generally describe, first, the scantling of the principal timbers, and then the fixing centres and the method of securing and bearing these joists.

13.12   Timber floor. The timber first floor shall be constructed from 225 x 50 mm sawn soft-wood joists (insert quality of timber, etc.) at 400 mm centres carried on and spiked to sheradized steel joist hangers as specified.

The quality of the material may be incorporated here or described specifically in the material clauses previously incorporated in the woodwork trade section. In addition the incorporation of herringbone strutting should be added.

13.13   Provide and fix to joists 50 x 38 mm sawn softwood herringbone strutting at centres not exceeding 1800 mm.

Covering the joists with either boarding or chipboard is a separate work item and would be described in a separate clause.

13.14   Boarded floors. Provide and fix to floor joists 19 mm p.t. & g. softwood boarding to BS 1297: 1970, the boards tightly cramped up and with each heading joint terminating over a supported joist. Each board to be twice nailed with 50 mm cut nails to each joist, the heads well punched home. Perform all cutting and fitting required including forming screwed access traps for electric ceiling lighting points under.

The location of these short work clauses and descriptions in the specification should follow the logical sequence of construction so far as this is possible, bearing in mind that work on a building in a particular trade is often not continuous but subject to starts and stops and unforeseen delays. The sequence selected should follow the ideal. This will be apparent from the examples given for specific work in the specifications which follow later in this book.

6 British Standard Specifications and Codes of Practice applicable to building works (as BSI list, November 1983)

While British Standard Specifications and Codes of Practice cover a very wide range of materials, standards of design and standards of workmanship relevant to the building industry, the extent to which they are applicable to any one job is often difficult to decide. In the main, these specifications refer to minimum acceptable standards and in many contracts higher standards would be normal accepted requirements. However, as a basis for minima, they can be used with confidence; higher standards can be built on those described in these documents. However, care must be taken to ensure that higher standards are, in fact, obtainable in present-day, highly commercial circumstances; if required they should be specifically described in specific work clauses.

Given that the BS and CPs provide reasonable working standards for normal commercial building works, the specification writer needs to be familiar with the standards themselves, especially as he will need to select the correct reference for his work. In practice the writer should refer to the BS for the more usual materials incorporated in buildings − cement, bricks, tiles, drainage goods, etc. − and to the CP for work where this would be suitable. In all instances Codes of Practice, as they are revised, will conform to the normal numbering system and their full title will become British Standard Code of Practice, so a careful check should be made before reference is made. The precise BS and CP must be quoted by number and date. It is not sufficient to merely incorporate in the preliminaries: 'All materials to be in accordance with the relevant British Standards Specifications', or 'All works are to be carried out strictly in accordance with the relevant Codes of Practice issued by the British Standards Institution'. In addition, as many BS are subdivided into parts, the correct part should be added to the title.

The following is a schedule of those British Standards Specifications and Codes of Practice in general use in building works. These are in appropriate trade form as set out in SMM6, published by the Royal Institution of Chartered Surveyors.

Demolition	BS 6187: 1982	Demolition
Excavation and earthwork	BS 5930: 1981	CP for site investigations
	BS 6031: 1981	Earthworks
	BS 1377: 1967	Methods of testing soils for engineering purposes
	BS 1924: 1975	Methods of test for stabilized soils

Piling and diaphragm walling	BS 5930: 1981 CP for site investigations CP 2004: 1972 Foundations

Concrete work

CP 101: 1972   Foundations and substructures
CP 110, Pt 1: 1972   The structural use of concrete (design, materials and workmanship)
CP 114, Pt 2: 1969   The structural use of reinforced concrete in buildings
CP 2004: 1972   Foundations
BS 12: 1978   Portland cement
BS 340: 1979   Precast concrete kerbs, edgings, etc.
BS 882, Pt 2: 1973   Aggregates from natural sources for concrete
BS 1521: 1972   Waterproof building papers
BS 5328: 1981   Methods for specifying concrete including ready-mixed concrete
BS 3148: 1980   Tests for water for making concrete
BS 4027: 1980   Sulphate resisting cements
BS 4449: 1978   Hot rolled steel bars for the reinforcement of concrete
BS 4461: 1978   Cold worked steelbars for the reinforcement of concrete
BS 4483: 1969   Steel fabric for the reinforcement of concrete
CP 116, Pt 2: 1969   The structural use of precast concrete
CP 116, Pt 2, Addendum No. 1: 1970   Large panel structures and structural connections in precast concrete

Brickwork and blockwork

CP 121, Pt 1: 1973   Walling of brick or blockwork
BS 12: 1978   Portland cement
BS 187: 1978   Calcium silicate bricks
BS 743: 1970   Materials for damp proof courses (bitumen based)
BS 890: 1972   Building limes
BS 1198, 1199, 1200: 1976   Building sands from natural sources
BS 1243: 1978   Metal ties for cavity wall construction
BS 6073, Pt 1: 1981   Precast concrete masonry units
BS 3921: 1974   Clay bricks
BS 493, Pt 2: 1970   Air bricks and gratings for wall ventilation

Rubble walling and Masonry

BS 6073, Pt 1: 1981   Precast concrete masonry units
BS 5977, Pt 1: 1982   Natural stone lintels
BS 2847: 1957   Glossary of terms for stone used in buildings
BS 3798: 1964   Copings (including cast and natural stone and slate)
BS 5642, Pt 1: 1978   Sills (including cast and natural stone and slate)
BS 5390: 1976   CP for stone masonry

Asphalt work   CP 144, Pt 4: 1970 Mastic asphalt (roof coverings)
BS 747: 1977 Roofing felts (black sheathing felt)
BS 988, 1076, 1097, 1451: 1973 Mastic asphalt for building (limestone aggregate)
BS 1162, 1410, 1418: 1973 Mastic asphalt for building (natual rock asphalt)
BS 6229: 1982 Code of practice for flat roofs with continuously supported coverings

Roofing   (*See* Asphalt for asphalt roofing and Woodwork for nails and fixings.)

BS 5268, Pt 5: 1977 Preservative treatment for constructional timber
CP 143, Pt 11: 1970 Sheet roof and wall coverings: Lead
CP 144, Pt 3: 1970 Built up bitumen felt
BS 402: 1979 Clay plain roofing tiles and fittings
BS 473, 550, Pt 2: 1971 Concrete roofing tiles and fittings
BS 680, Pt 2: 1971 Roofing slates (natural)
BS 690, Pt 2: 1974 Asbestos cement slates
BS 747: 1977 Roofing felts
BS 1178: 1982 Milled lead sheet and strip for building purposes
BS 2717: 1956 Glossary of terms applicable to roof coverings
BS 4072: 1974 Wood preservative by water borne compositions
BS 4471, Pt 2: 1971 Small resawn sections (tiling battens)

CP 143: *Sheet roof and wall coverings*
CP 143, Pt 5: 1964 Zinc (Imperial)
BS 3083: 1980 Galvanised corrugated steel
CP 143, Pt 11: 1970 Lead
CP 143, Pt 12: 1970 Copper
BS 4868: 1972 Aluminium profiled sheet

BS 849: 1939 Plain zinc sheet roofing
BS 1178: 1982 Milled sheet lead and strip
BS 1470: 1972 Wrot aluminium plate, sheet and strip
BS 2870: 1980 Rolled copper sheet, strip and foil
BS 5534, Pt 1: 1978 CP for slating and tiling

Woodwork   BS 5268, Pt 5: 1977 Preservative treatment for constructional timber
CP 112, Pt 2: 1971 The structural use of timber
CP 112, Pt 3: 1973 Trussed rafters for the roofs of dwellings
CP 201, Pt 2: 1972 Timber flooring
BS 589, 881: 1974 Nomenclature of commercial timbers
BS 1142, Pt 2: 1971 Medium board and hardboard
BS 1142, Pt 3: 1972 Insulating board
BS 1186, Pt 1: 1971 Quality of timber in joinery
BS 4951: 1973 Builders hardware (locks and latches)

BS 1186, Pt 2: 1971   Quality of workmanship in joinery
BS 1202, Pt 1: 1974   Steel nails
BS 1202, Pt 2: 1974   Copper nails
BS 1202, Pt 3: 1974   Aluminium nails
BS 1210: 1963   Wood screws
BS 1227, Pt 1A: 1967   Hinges for general building purposes
BS 1331: 1954   Builders hardware for housing
BS 1455: 1972   Plywood . . . from tropical hardwoods
BS 1494, Pt 1: 1964   Fixings for sheet roof coverings, etc.
BS 1494, Pt 2: 1967   Coach and handrail screws, etc.
BS 2604, Pt 2: 1970   Resin bonded wood chipboard
BS 3444: 1972   Blockboard and laminboard
BS 3827: *Glossary of hardware terms*
BS 3827, Pt 1: 1964   Locks
BS 3827, Pt 2: 1967   Latches
BS 3827, Pt 3: 1967   Catches
BS 3827, Pt 4: 1967   Furniture
BS 4047: 1966   Grading rules for sawn home-grown hardwood
BS 4072: 1974   Wood preservative by water borne compositions
BS 4190: 1967   Black hexagonal bolts, screws and nuts
BS 4471, Pt 1: 1969   Dimensions for softwood
BS 4978: 1973   Timber grades for structural use
CP 151, Pt 1: 1957   Wooden doors
BS 459: *Wooden doors*
BS 459, Pt 1: 1954   Panelled and glazed
BS 459, Pt 2: 1962   Flush
BS 459, Pt 3: 1951   Firecheck flush, etc.
BS 459, Pt 4: 1965   Matchboarded doors
BS 644: *Wood windows*
BS 644, Pt 1: 1951   Wood casement windows
BS 644, Pt 2: 1958   Wood double hung sash windows
BS 644, Pt 3: 1951   Wood double hung sash windows and case windows (Scottish type)
BS 1285: 1980   Wood surrounds for steel windows and doors
BS 584: 1967   Wood trim (softwood)
BS 585: 1972   Wood stairs
BS 1195, Pt 2: 1972   Kitchen fitments and equipment

Structural steelwork

BS 5493: 1977   Corrosion protection
BS 4, Pt 1: 1980   Structural steel sections (hot rolled)
BS 6363: 1983   Welded cold formed steel structural sections
BS 449, Pt 2: 1969   The use of structural steel in building
Supplement No. 1 (1959) to BS 449, Pt 1: 1970 (PD 3343 Recommendations for design)
BS 6323, Pt 1: 1982   Steel tubes for . . . structural . . . purposes

BS 6323, Pt 8: 1982   Stainless steel tubes for . . . structural . . . purposes
BS 4360: 1979   Weldable structural steels
BS 4395: *High strength friction grip bolts, etc.*
BS 4395, Pt 1: 1969   General grade
BS 4395, Pt 2: 1969   Higher grade

Metalwork

(*See also* Structural steelwork.)

BS 5516: 1977   Patent glazing
BS 493, Pt 2: 1970   Airbrick and gratings for wall ventilation
BS 990, Pt 2: 1972   Steel windows (domestic)
BS 4951: 1973   Builders hardware
BS 1422: 1956   Steel subframes, etc., for metal windows
BS 1494: 1951   Fixing accessories for building purposes
BS 1787: 1951   Steel windows (industrial)
BS 2503: 1954   Steel windows (agricultural)
BS 2569, Pt 1: 1964   Sprayed metal coatings
BS 4092, Pt 1: 1966   Metal gates
BS 4190: 1967   Black hexagonal bolts, etc.
BS 4229, Pt 2: 1969   Metric sizes of ferrous bars
BS 4449: 1978   Hot rolled steel bars
BS 4461: 1978   Cold worked steel bars
BS 4592: 1970   Industrial type open metal flooring and stair treads
BS 325: 1947   Black cup and countersunk head bolts, etc.
BS 5493: 1977   CP for protective coating of iron . . . etc.

Plumbing and mechanical engineering services

Rainwater services

CP 308: 1974   Drainage of roofs and paved areas
BS 460: 1964   Cast iron rainwater goods
BS 569: 1973   Asbestos cement rainwater goods
BS 1091: 1963   Pressed steel gutters, etc.
BS 1431: 1960   Wrot copper and zinc rainwater goods
BS 2997: 1958   Aluminium rainwater goods
BS 4576, Pt 1: 1970   uPVC rainwater goods (half round gutters and circular pipes)

Cold water services and sanitary plumbing

CP 99: 1972   Frost precautions for water services

CP 305, Pt 1: 1974   Selection and installation (of) sanitary appliances

CP 310: 1965   Water supply

BS 1010, Pt 2: 1973   Draw off taps and stop valves

BS 1184: 1976   Copper and copper alloy traps

BS 1387: 1967   Steel tubes for screwing to BS 21 pipe threads

BS 5154: 1974   Copper alloy gate valves

BS 2871, Pt 2: 1972   Copper and copper alloy tubes

BS 3505: 1968   uPVC pipe for cold water services

BS 5153: 1974   Cast iron check valves for general purposes

BS 417, Pt 2: 1973   Galvanised m.s. cisterns and cylinders

BS 1212, Pt 1: 1953   Ball valves — piston type

BS 1212, Pt 2: 1970   Ball valves — diaphragm type

BS 1212, Pt 3: 1979   Plastic body

BS 1968: 1953   Floats for ball valves (copper)

BS 2456: 1973   Floats for ball valves (plastic)

BS 2777: 1974   Asbestos cement cisterns

BS 4213: 1975   Polyolefin . . . C/w storage cisterns

BS 699: 1972   Copper cylinders (direct)

BS 1566, Pt 1: 1972   Copper indirect cylinders (double feed)

BS 1566, Pt 2: 1972   Copper indirect cylinders (single feed)

BS 416: 1973   Cast iron spigot and socket waste and vent pipes

BS 2760: 1973   Pitch-impregnated fibre pipes and fittings

BS 5255: 1976   Plastic waste traps and pipes

BS 4515: 1983   uPVC soil and vent pipes

BS 5572: 1978   Sanitary pipework above ground

BS 1189: 1972   Cast iron baths

BS 1390: 1972   Sheet steel baths

BS 3380: 1982   Wastes and bath overflows

BS 4305: 1972   Baths . . . from acrylic sheet

BS 1188: 1974   Ceramic washbasins and pedestals

BS 1329: 1974   Metal lavatory basins

BS 1125: 1973   WC flushing cisterns

BS 5503, Pt 2: 1977   Ceramic washdown WC pans

BS 1206: 1974   Fireclay sinks

BS 1244, Pt 2: 1972   Metal sinks for domestic purposes

BS 1876: 1972   Automatic flushing cisterns for urinals

BS 4880, Pt 1: 1972   Stainless steel slab urinals

BS 5520: 1977   Bowl urinals

BS 4127, Pt 2: 1972   Light gauge stainless steel tubes

Hot water services

(*See also* Cold water services for cylinders, pipework, fittings and valves.)

Boilers and flues

CP 131: 1974   Flues for domestic appliances (solid fuel)
BS 5440, Pt 1: 1978   Flues for gas appliances up to 60 kW rating
BS 41: 1973   Cast iron spigot and socket flue pipes
BS 715: 1970   Sheet metal flue pipes for gas fired appliances
BS 835: 1973   Asbestos cement flue pipes, heavy quality
BS 759: 1975   Valves, gauges, etc., for boilers
BS 779: 1976   Cast iron boilers for central heating and hot water supply
BS 799, Pt 2: 1981   Oil burning equipment — vapourizing burners
BS 799, Pt 3: 1981   Automatic and semi-automatic atomizing burners
BS 799, Pt 4: 1972   Atomizing burners over 36 litres/hour
BS 855: 1976   Welded steel boilers for central heating and hot water supply
BS 2790: 1982   Welded steel boilers Class I
BS 4433, Pt 1: 1973   Solid fuel boilers with undergrate ash removal
BS 4433, Pt 2: 1969   Solid fuel boilers with gravity feed up to 45 kW
BS 3958: *Thermal insulating materials (for pipework)*
BS 3958, Pt 1: 1982   Magnesium preformed insulation
BS 3958, Pt 2: 1982   Calcium silicate preformed insulation
BS 3958, Pt 4: 1982   Bonded preformed mineral wool pipe sections
BS 3958, Pt 6: 1972   Finishing materials for site application to insulating materials

Heating

Low-pressure hot water

(*See also* Cold and Hot water services.)
BS 2767: 1972   Valves and unions for hot water radiators
BS 3528: 1977   Convector type space heaters (radiators)
BS 3955, Pt 3: 1979   Room thermostats

Gas space heaters

BS 5864: 1980   Ducted warm air systems
BS 570: 1959   Plug and socket connectors
BS 669: 1960   Flexible tubing and connectors
BS 5871: 1980   Space heating appliances
BS 3561: 1962   Non-domestic space heaters

Ventilation

BS 3456, Section 2.29: 1971   Ventilating fans
BS 4856, Pt 1: 1972   Fan coil units, unit heaters and coolers

Gas and *water mains*	(*See also* Cold water services.)
Gas	CP 331: *Installations of pipes and meters for town gas* CP 331, Pt 2: 1974 Metering and meter control CP 331, Pt 3: 1974 Low pressure installation pipes
Water	CP 99: 1972 Frost precautions for water services

Electrical installations

CP 1013: 1965   Earthing
BS 52: 1963   Bayonet lamp holders, etc.
BS 67: 1969   Ceiling roses
BS 3999, Pt 2: 1967   Thermal storage water heaters
BS 1363: 1967   13A plugs, socket outlets and boxes
BS 3052: 1958   Electric shaver supply units
BS 3456, Section 2.7: 1970   Water heaters
BS 3456, Section 2.21: 1972   Electric immersion heaters
BS 3676: 1963   Switches
BS 4177: 1967   Cooker control units
BS 4568, Pts 1, 2: 1970   Steel conduit and fittings
BS 4607, Pt 1: 1970   Rigid PVC conduits and fittings
BS 4662: 1970   Boxes for enclosure of electrical accessories
BS 4678, Pt 1: 1971   Cable trunking (steel surface)
BS 6004: 1975   PVC insulated cables
BS 6500: 1975   Insulated flexible cords
BS 5839, Pt 1: 1980   CP for installation and servicing fire protection services
BS 3955, Pt 3: 1979   Electrical controls for household . . . purposes (thermostats, etc.)

Floor, wall and ceiling finishes

Pavings

CP 201, Pt 2: 1972   Wood flooring (board, strip, block, mosaic)
CP 202: 1972   Tile and slab flooring
CP 203, Pt 2: 1972   Sheet and tile flooring (cork, linoleum, plastics, rubber)
CP 204, Pt 2: 1970   Insitu floor finishes (pitch mastic, magnesite, cement, terrazzo)
BS 776, Pt 2: 1972   Materials for magnesium oxychloride (magnesite) flooring
BS 810: 1966   Sheet linoleum and linoleum tiles
BS 1187: 1959   Wood blocks for floors
BS 1286: 1974   Clay tiles for flooring

BS 1297: 1970   Grading and sizing of softwood flooring
BS 1711: 1975   Solid rubber flooring
BS 1863: 1952   Felt backed linoleum
BS 2592: 1973   Thermoplastic flooring tiles
BS 3620: 1969   PVC (vinyl) asbestos floor tiles
BS 3261, Pt 1: 1973   Unbacked flexible PVC flooring
BS 4050, Pt 2: 1966   Wood mosaic flooring
BS 4131: 1973   Terrazzo tiles

*Plastering,
wall tiling
and terrazzo*

(*See also* Concrete for sands and cement; Brickwork for hydraulic lime.)
BS 5385, Pt 1: 1976   Internal ceramic wall tiling
BS 5385, Pt 2: 1978   External ceramic wall tiling and mosaics
BS 1191, Pt 1: 1973   Gypsum plaster
BS 1191, Pt 2: 1973   Gypsum plaster, pre-mixed lightweight grades
BS 1230: 1970   Gypsum plasterboard
BS 1281: 1974   Glazed ceramic tiles and fittings for internal walls
BS 1369: 1947   Metal lathing (steel) for plastering
BS 4049: 1966   Glossary of terms for plastering, etc.
BS 4131: 1973   Terrazzo tiles
BS 5492: 1977   Internal plastering

Glazing

BS 6262: 1982   Glazing and fixing of glass
BS 5516: 1977   Patent glazing
BS 544: 1969   Linseed oil putty for . . . wood frame
BS 952, Pt 1: 1978   Glass for glazing
BS 3447: 1962   Glossary of terms used in glass industry
BS 5713: 1979   Specification for hermetically sealed flat double glazing units

**Painting and
decorating**

BS 6150: 1982   Painting of buildings
BS 5493: 1977   Cleaning and preparation of metal surfaces
BS 242, 243, 259, 632: 1969   Linseed oil
BS 1336: 1971   Knotting
BS 2015: 1965   Glossary of paint terms
BS 2523: 1966   Lead based priming paint
BS 3046: 1981   Paperhanging pastes and powders
BS 3416: 1975   Black bitumen coating solutions for cold application
BS 3698: 1964   Calcium plumbate priming paints

BS 4652: 1971   Metallic zinc-rich priming paints
BS 4756: 1971   Aluminium priming paint for woodwork
BS 4764: 1971   Powder cement paints

Drainage   CP 301: 1971   Building drainage
BS 6297: 1983   Small sewerage treatment works
BS 65: 1981   Clay drain and sewer pipes and fittings
BS 6087: 1981   Flexible mechanical joints
BS 437: 1978   Cast iron drain pipes and fittings
BS 497: 1976   Cast iron manhole covers, gulley grating and frames
BS 5911: 1981   Concrete pipes and fittings, manholes, gullies, etc.
BS 1194: 1969   Concrete porous pipes for subsoil drainage
BS 1196: 1971   Clayware field drain pipes
BS 2760: 1973   Pitch fibre drain pipes and fittings
BS 4460: 1973   uPVC drain pipes and fittings
BS 4962: 1982   Plastic pipe for sub-soil drainage

Fencing, etc.   BS 340: 1979   Precast concrete kerbs, edgings, etc.
BS 1722, Pt 1: 1972   Chain link fences
BS 1722, Pt 2: 1973   Woven wire fences
BS 1722, Pt 3: 1973   Strained wire fences
BS 1722, Pt 4: 1972   Cleft chestnut pale fences
BS 1722, Pt 5: 1972   Close boarded fences . . .
BS 1722, Pt 6: 1972   Wooden palisade fences
BS 1722, Pt 7: 1972   Wooden post and rail fences
BS 1722, Pt 8: 1978   Mild steel or wrot iron . . . bar fences
BS 1722, Pt 9: 1979   Mild steel or wrot iron unclimbable fences . . .
BS 1722, Pt 10: 1972   Anti-intruder chain link fences
BS 1722, Pt 11: 1972   Woven wood fences
BS 4102: 1971   Steel wire for fences
BS 3470: 1975   Field gates and posts
BS 4092, Pt 1: 1966   Metal gates
BS 4092, Pt 2: 1966   Wooden gates

7 General contract and preliminary clauses

All building specifications, whether for new or alteration works, have two main types of clauses:

1   those which describe the general conditions under which the work will be carried out, the various obligations which both employer and contractor will be required to observe and the duties and limitations of the architect;

2   those in which the materials and workmanship are described in detail and where the specific work clauses amplify the drawings and details.

In the preparation of a specification it is usual to follow generally accepted practice and commence the document with the first group of clauses incorporating details of the contract form which it is proposed to use. It is advisable to provide a heading to the specification describing the type of works to be carried out, the address or location of the site or building and the name of the employer. It is also usual to incorporate the name and address of the architect although this is often added at the end of the specification. Many architects sign their specifications; where this is the practice, the name usually appears on the last page before the schedule of Provisional and Prime Cost Sums. Alternative forms of heading are:

Specification of works to be carried out and materials to be used in alterations and extensions to Bray's Hill Farm, Ashburnham, near Battle, East Sussex, for Arnside Properties Ltd to the reasonable satisfaction of the architect.

June 1973

Specification of works to be carried out and materials to be used in the erection and completion of a new house and garage on Plot 8 Selmeston Drive, Seaford, East Sussex, for B.G. Smith, Esq., to the reasonable satisfaction of the architect.

Ivor Brown, RIBA
Chartered Architect

July 1975

It is immaterial which form is used so long as the required information is incorporated.

The general conditions of contract which follow the heading should commence by describing precisely the form of contract that will be used. This description must incorporate the full title of the document, the issuing authority and the date of issue, and the date of the latest revision. There are occasions when it may be necessary to vary the contract conditions slightly to conform to the requirements either of the work or the employer. Any variations must be fully described in this section of the specification; it is wise to draw the contractor's attention to these and advise him that specification clauses take precedence over the standard contract form to be employed.

Finally, a clause in this section should incorporate precise details of matters over which the architect is empowered to exercise options on behalf of the employer. These include sums for liquidated and ascertained damages, defects liability period and similar matters. These options must be crystallized into specific sums and periods of time and shown against the respective contract clause numbers inserted in the specification.

The second part of the preliminary clauses deals with a number of matters pertaining to the organization and running of the contract which affect in some way the preparation of the tender and the management of the works. These vary somewhat between the different types of specification, and specifications for alteration works also differ somewhat from new works specifications. In addition, specifications for works involving finance from statutory grants require a number of additional clauses to cover specific requirements of the statutory authority responsible for discharging payments under the relevant legislation.

The clauses incorporated in this chapter covering general conditions and preliminaries show alternatives for alteration and new works together with specific clauses required for specifications for works carried out under improvement grants. In addition, notes are appended describing reasons for the form and inclusion of each clause.

This clause advises the contractor that the works will be carried out under a formal contractural arrangement.

The form of contract is here described in full (an alternative form for larger or longer contracts is given later). It is important to describe precisely the edition concerned and its date.

Specifications sometimes incorporate clauses which are at variance with contract clauses: this makes it clear which takes precedence.

In the Agreement for Minor Building Works there are a number of clauses which must be deleted, or in which information must be inserted or alternatives selected. As these will affect the contractors estimate, full details must be inserted in the general conditions of the specification so that the contractors are under no misapprehension as to these matters. Each contract will be slightly different and the specification writer must obtain from the architect the relevant information.

In the Intermediate Form of Building Contract as with the other forms of contract, certain amendments to the text must be made and certain clauses need to be deleted or information inserted or alternatives selected.

1.00   GENERAL CONDITIONS

1.01   <u>Contract form.</u> The contractor shall be required to enter into a contract for the due and proper completion of the works.

1.02   The agreement and schedule of conditions of building contract shall be the Agreement for Minor Building Works issued by the Joint Contracts Tribunal, first issued January 1980.

1.03   Where clauses in this specification are at variance with the form of contract, the clause in this specification shall be binding.

1.04   The following amendments will be made to or incorporated in the Agreement:
  (a) The words 'Supervising Officer' (Architect) shall be deleted from the Agreement.
  (b) Recitals (identify deletions as instructed)
      Clause 2.1   (insert date for possession)
               (insert date for completion)
      Clause 2.3   (insert amount per week)
      Clause 2.5   (insert period other than three months)
      Clause 4.1   (advise deletions as instructed – see recitals on page 1)
      Clause 4.2   (adjust retention percentage if other than 5 per cent)
      Clause 4.3   (adjust percentage if that in 4.2 has been adjusted)
      Clause 4.4   (insert period if other than three months)
      Clause 4.5   (to be deleted if period of contract is of limited duration or as instructed)
      Clause 5.5   (to be deleted unless employer is local authority)
      Clause 6.3   (delete either A or B as applicable. If 6.3A is retained then insert required percentage as instructed)

   An alternative contract form could be described in the General Conditions as follows, after Clause 1.01 as previously drafted.

1.02   The agreement and schedule of conditions of building contract shall be the Intermediate Form of Building Contract, 1984 Edition, issued by the Joint Contracts Tribunal (IFC 84).

1.03   (as before)

1.04   The following amendments and inclusions will be made to or incorporated in the Agreement:

It should be remembered that in specifications using IFC, Prime Cost Sums cannot be used in the Specification and Provisional Sums required the insertion of the firm and person named.

In the Standard Form of Building Contract, as with the Agreement for Minor Building Works, certain clauses need to be deleted or information must be inserted or alternatives selected.

(a) The words 'Architect' or 'Supervising Officer' will be deleted throughout as appropriate.

(b) Recitals (identify deletions and/or amendments as instructed)

1st (b)	delete 'the Specification/the Schedules of Work/Bills of Quantities' as appropriate
(c)	delete if appropriate
(d)	delete either 2A or B as appropriate
2nd A(b)	delete as appropriate

(c) Appendix

Article 5.1	Appointment of arbitrator (delete as appropriate)
5.3	
5.4	
Clause 2.1	(insert date of possession) (insert date for completion)
Clause 2.4.10	Extension of time (delete as appropriate)
2.4.11	
Clause 2.2	Deferrment of date for possession (delete if not applicable and
2.4.14	insert period if applicable not exceeding six weeks)
4.11(a)	
Clause 2.7	Liquidated damages (insert rate at £ per week)
Clause 2.10	Defects liability period (insert period if other than six months)
Clause 4.2	Period of interim payments (insert period if other than one month)
Clause 4.5	Period of final measurement (insert period if other than six months)
Clause 4.9	Supplement Condition C (insert percentage)
D1	
Clause 6.2.1	Insurance cover: third party (insert limit of cover)
Clause 6.3	Insurance against Clause 6.3 perils: fire (delete as appropriate)
Clause 6.3A.1	Percentage to cover professional fees (insert percentage)
Clause 8.3	Date of tender (insert date ten days before date for receipt of tenders by employer)

An alternative contract form could be described in the General Conditions as follows, after Clause 1.01 as previously drafted.

1.02   The agreement and schedule of conditions of building contract shall be the Standard Form of Building Contract, 1980 Edition, Private without Quantities issued by the Joint Contracts Tribunal.

1.03   (as before)

1.04   The following amendments and inclusions will be made to or incorporated in the Agreement:

Article 4A	(delete if no Quantity Surveyor appointed)
Article 5.5	(adjust for contract works outside England and Wales where English law does not apply)

This clause is generally inserted only for improvement work to existing properties where the cost of the work is to be grant aided. It enables the tender to be easily separated into 'improvements' and 'repairs' so that the value of improvements can be readily computed.

The paragraph dealing with the provision of a separate estimate covering VAT is applicable to all specifications prepared for alteration and repair work under existing legislation.

This clause is inserted only for improvement work to existing properties where the cost of the work is to be grant aided.

This clause is applicable to all building specifications for work where subcontracting is likely.

	Clause 5.3.1.2	(delete if instructed)
	Clause 5.3.2	(amended if deletion above is incorporated)
	Clause 22	(delete Clauses 22A, 22B or 22C as applicable to particular contract works)
Appendix	Clause 1.3	Date for completion (insert)
	Clause 17.2	Defects liability period (state if other than six months)
	Clause 21.1.1	(state amount)
	Clause 22A	(state unless clause deleted)
	Clause 23.1	Date for possession (insert)
	Clause 24.2	(state at rate per week)
	Clause 28.1.3.2	(state three months)
	Clause 28.1.3.1 Clause 28.1.3.3– Clause 28.1.3.7	(state one month)
	Clause 30.1.3	(state monthly unless agreed otherwise)
	Clause 30.4.1.1	(retention: state if less than 5 per cent)
	Clause 30.6.1.2	(period of final measurement – state if other than six months)
	Clause 37	(fluctuations: delete either 38 or 39)

2.00 PRELIMINARIES

2.01 Estimates. Contractors should acquaint themselves with the conditions of work before tendering as no claim will be entertained on the grounds of want of knowledge.

Estimates are to be submitted exclusive of Value Added Tax. A separate estimate of anticipated VAT chargeable on repairs, works and equipment supplied is to be attached to the form of tender.

All items described herein, to which a tenderer attaches a monetary value, shall be entered either under the 'improvements' or 'repairs' columns or apportioned between both columns as appropriate.

Tenders are subject to the approval of the. . . . (Greater London Council and/or Housing Corporation and/or local authority).

2.02 Financing Authority. Finance for the work is provided from funds and/or grants released by the . . . . (Greater London Council/Housing Corporation/local authority or a combination of these authorities), hereafter referred to as the Financing Authority (or FA).

2.03 Finance (No. 2) Act 1975. The contractor shall comply with Sections 68 to 71 and Schedules 12 and 13 of the Finance (No. 2) Act 1975.

The contractor shall satisfy the employer, prior to signing the contract, that he holds an appropriate subcontractor's certificate from the Inland Revenue and he shall not employ any subcontractor, whether nominated or otherwise, who does not possess such a certificate.

For the purpose of this Act the employers are a 'contractor' at the the time of the tender.

This clause is designed to draw the contractor's attention to his responsibilities when preparing his tender and to warn him that he must satisfy himself on the limitations and problems which he will encounter. With specifications for alteration works, the brackets are omitted.

This clause covers the employer against police action for careless placing of skips, materials, scaffolding and rubbish from the works where existing buildings are being altered.

Where trial holes have been excavated on site, the contractor's attention should be drawn both to them and any information shown on the drawings. It is his responsibility under this clause to examine the holes on site and obtain his own information and draw his own conclusions as to the nature of the subsoil and subsoil conditions.

This clause spells out both the general conditions regarding the works and indicates to the contractor that he will be responsible both for all items required for the works and for its protection and security for the period of the contract.

This clause places the responsibility for protection of the works from inclement weather and the effects of frost for the period of the contract.

With works to existing buildings, generally water is available on site from the water company's main for the use of the contractor. This clause instructs him to carry out all works necessary to bring the water to a suitable position for use and include for all costs and charges in his tender.

With new works where water is not available, the contractor must arrange for a supply and include for all charges levied by the water supply authority. The size required for the new mains connection must be incorporated in the clause.

A dirty site is a dangerous site and not to be tolerated. Rubbish should be regularly cleared away and the site left clean on completion.

This clause restricts the contractor's use of a site or building to the area of the works or as shown.

This clause saves a great deal of explanatory text in a specification and indicates precisely to the contractor what his tender must include in such works.

2.04 Visit site. The contractor shall visit the site of the works to acquaint himself with the nature of the work to be carried out, the approach to the site (and the nature of the existing structure), as no claim will be recognized on grounds of want of knowledge of the works involved.

2.05 Police regulations. The contractor shall comply with police regulations and, in particular, keep the highway and footpath unobstructed and free from materials or debris arising from the works.

2.06 Trial holes. Where trial holes have been provided, their position on the site and details of subsoil exposed will be indicated on the drawings. The contractor, however, shall in any event make his own investigation as no claim will be entertained through the subsoil varying from that indicated on the trial hole section.

2.07 Works to be considered new, except where specified to the contrary and as including all labour, materials, package, cartage, risk, unloading, storage under cover where required, moving, locating, hoisting and fixing in the required positions and the use of all tools, implements, tackle, scaffolding and all other plant, tarpaulins, the temporary enclosure of openings and other items for the works and the use of workmen and for the protection and security of the structure.

2.08 Inclement weather. During wet or frosty weather all exposed portions of the works shall be properly protected.

2.09 Water. For works involving the alteration or extension of existing structures, unless specified to the contrary, water will be available on site for the use of the contractor who shall execute all temporary plumbing and provide necessary storage and pay all costs, charges and fees for water levied by the water board for building purposes.
     Alternative clause for *new works:*
The contractor shall make all arrangements with the water board to provide a new (size) main connection complete to the boundary of the site and pay all costs, charges and fees for the work and for water levied by the water board for building purposes.

2.10 Keep site clean. The contractor shall clear and cart away from site all rubbish and debris as it accumulates and on completion of the works leave the site clean, neat and tidy to the reasonable satisfaction of the architect.

2.11 Access. Access to the works or site shall be restricted as shown on the drawings or specified hereafter.

2.12 Making good. All 'making good' or 'making out' which becomes necessary after the removal of any part of the structure or other causes contingent to the works will be complete and to match the surrounding work in all respects, except where specified to the contrary.

The contractor is required to organize and manage the work. This clause gives him authority to give such notices and pay such fees as are required by statutory and other authorities.

This clause ensures that copies of all information required for the proper running of the contract are available to the contractor's representatives on site.

An invaluable aid to small works contracts, the instruction book should be covered in all specifications and made use of in project management.

Dayworks are a perennial problem on all building contracts despite the requirements of the JCT Form of Contract clauses. This clause spells out clearly to the contractor what will be permitted by the architect.

This clause enforces the use of the standard form of contract between building employers and subcontractors. It also spells out the basic attendance requirements and places responsibility on the contractor to agree working details, etc., with the subcontractors.

This short clause requires the contractor to include in his tender for all fixings and small fittings and labours necessary for the completion of the specified works.

This clause must be inserted when the Intermediate Form of Contract is used.

This definition is inserted to simplify the use of the expression and to break down its use between 'materials and service' and 'material only' items.

An explanatory clause to define precisely what is required of the contractor when these terms are incorporated in 'work clauses'.

A general clause to cover these statutory payments.

A general clause to amplify the contractor's duties (see also Clause 2.10) for handing over the building in a clean and satisfactory condition.

The incorporation of a contingency sum to cover unforeseen eventualities is necessary in all building contracts. The sum can be as low as 5 per cent of the estimated value of the works and can rise to 20 per cent in complicated works to historic buildings. The architect will specify the sum to be included.

2.13   Notices. The contractor shall give all notices to the local authority, county surveyor, water board, electricity and gas boards as required and appropriate and pay all fees legally demandable.

2.14   Drawings. A full set of drawings, a copy of this specification and copies of all Architect's Instructions and nominated subcontract and suppliers' tenders shall be kept on site for use and reference.

2.15   Site instruction book. The contractor shall supply and keep on site a quarto triplicate notebook in which to record all site queries and site instructions. At the end of each month the contractor will forward one copy of each page of queries and instructions to the architect for the issue of a formal instruction.

2.16   Dayworks. Dayworks will only be permitted on the specific written instructions of the architect. All daywork charges are to be compiled using the Prime Cost of Dayworks (as defined and published by the RICS and NFBTE), and the percentages inserted by the contractor on the Form of Tender or the accompanying Schedule of Rates, which percentages will be incorporated in the Appendix to the Contract and the Schedule of Rates appended.

2.17   Subcontractors. The contractor shall enter into agreements with his subcontractors embodying the same conditions for which he himself is responsible. Provide attendance, including free use of scaffolding, plant, lighting, power and water. The contractor shall agree all working details and dimensions with subcontractors.

2.18   Estimating. The contractor shall include in his tender for everything necessary to complete the works within the time and reasonable intention of this specification and drawings.

2.19   Fair Wages. The contractor shall pay rates of wages and observe hours and conditions of labour not less favourable than those established for the trade or industry in the district where the work is carried out.

2.20   Prime Cost Sums. For convenient reference, 'Prime Cost' is used to identify services to be carried out by a nominated subcontractor, a statutory undertaking or a public authority, and the abbreviation 'PC' is used to identify materials or goods to be obtained from a nominated supplier.

2.21   Interpretation of terms. The terms 'fix', 'fit', 'lay', etc., shall be interpreted as 'provide and fix', 'provide and fit', etc., and the terms 'as directed' and 'as approved' to be interpreted 'as directed by the architect' and 'to the approval of the architect'.

2.22   Insurance. The contractor shall pay all contributions required under the National Health and Insurance Scheme.

2.23   Cleaning. The contractor shall include in his tender for thoroughly cleaning all floors and pavings included in or affected by the works, sanitary fittings, gullies, gutters, cesspools and glazing both sides on completion and leaving all clean and perfect to the reasonable satisfaction of the architect.

2.24   Contingency sum. Include the Provisional Sum of £＿＿＿＿ for contingencies, to be expended on the architect's instructions if required and deducted wholly or in part from the contract sum if not required.

8 Specifications for new works

Building specifications for new works (where quantities do not form a part of the contract) are contract documents and as such play a vital part in expanding the architect's ideas and requirements, which have only been indicated in basic form on the drawings and details. It is therefore important that the specification writer fully appreciates this function as the contractor will continuously turn to the specification for information.

In Chapter 1, we saw that the specification is used primarily by the estimator, in conjunction with the drawings, to enable him to prepare his estimate, and by the supervising staff to interpret the architect's intentions in respect of materials and workmanship. In minor works contracts where no quantities are provided the specification is required for precisely the same reasons. The document should therefore be prepared with these objects in view.

A specification for new works where no quantities are provided will be prepared in accordance with the following pattern:

(a) General conditions and contract form which has been fully described in Chapter 7.

(b) Preliminary clauses, which have also been fully described in Chapter 7. Clauses for new works should be selected from the examples given, excluding those specifically for specifications covering alteration works and those specifically for improvement grant contracts.

(c) Workmanship and material clauses separated into the different trade sections. These trade sections for a number of years have followed a pattern which can be seen in the familiar works described in the Introduction. The publication in 1979 of SMM6 has radically altered both the nomenclature and arrangement of the trade clauses in bills of quantities; these have been incorporated in the examples in this chapter.

Sections (a) and (b) (contract form and preliminaries) of a specification for new works then follow the patterns described in Chapter 7, the clauses relating to the form of contract and general preliminaries being selected, and additional clauses to suit particular situations drafted and inserted as required.

Section (c) forms the bulk of the specification. Generally it is found practical to commence each trade section with a number of clauses describing the particular materials selected for use. These clauses must define or expand precisely the architect's requirements and should incorporate the following information as applicable:

the size, overall dimensions or type reference of the material or article (e.g. structural steelwork) its consistency or material from which it is manufactured (e.g. ironmongery)

its colour or texture (e.g. bricks)

the manufacturer or supplier, preferably incorporating the address and full details (e.g. roofing slates)

applicable BS number and reference relating to such materials or components as are covered and available through general material suppliers (e.g. standard wood or metal windows)

Not every clause will require all of these but all will require at least one if not more to provide sufficient information. Following the material clauses will be a number of workmanship clauses, each describing in some detail the particular requirements for the various labours in order to produce the quality and finish to the trade works expressly required by the architect. There are two principal methods by which these requirements are drawn to the contractor's attention:

1   by incorporating reference to a BS Code of Practice for the specific trade or work involved;

2   by describing in full or appropriate detail the specific requirements of each area of work.

The problem with using Codes of Practice to cover the quality of workmanship is that, while some are generally understood and their provisions form a part of usual good trade practice, others are not. Not all builders (or even architects), own or are aware of the details and implications of these codes; this is particularly true of smaller contractors who carry out most 'minor works' contracts, which are the bulk of building work today. However, these contractors and their staff do understand the generally accepted norms written into the traditional workmanship clauses, which form a large part of specifications written for the building industry.

Workmanship clauses, therefore, can be divided into two types: first, those which incorporate where applicable, Codes of Practice in specific trade situations where the Codes are the accepted method of working; second, in other trade areas, those which incorporate the traditional descriptions understood by the contractors and their staff who are required to carry out the work.

The following suggested clauses are for the erection and completion of a detached dwelling and garage, a common contract in general practice. The trade sections have been laid out in accordance with the sequence incorporated in SMM6; while not all relevant trades or materials have been included, there should be enough to show how a specification for such a project could be prepared.

The general conditions of contract and preliminary clauses will generally follow the form suggested, amended as necessary to meet the particular requirements of individual contract works.

Demolition works generally follow on spot item format as shown. The works may include building demolition, throwing, grubbing out and clearing trees, breaking out drains and basements. In specific cases, the contractor may be instructed to leave approved hardcore on site to a specified quantity; the precise specification for permissible quality, and the hardcore's position on site, must be incorporated.

Topsoil from site strip can be deposited in a spoil heap on site for future garden works. Position should be described or indicated on site plan.

General clauses for excavation of foundation trenches, water mains and drainage separated into sections. Gas and electricity boards carry out their own trenchwork. Trenches under pavings should be broken in at the top to reduce problems of filling settlement.

The type of hardcore available varies with different districts. Brick hardcore is scarce and expensive; in some areas crushed top beds from local quarries are an alternative. Ballast 'as dug', chalk and hoggin are also used. In extreme cases of shortage weak-mix concrete may be specified.

Specification of works to be carried out and materials to be used in the erection and completion of a new house and garage on Plot No. 9, Glynde Drive, Seacombe, Sussex, for D.S. James, Esq., to the reasonable satisfaction of the architect.

Ivor Brown, RIBA
Chartered Architect

September 1977

1.00   GENERAL CONDITIONS
(See Chapter 7.)

2.00   PRELIMINARIES
(See Chapter 7.)

3.00   DEMOLITION

3.01   Carefully demolish existing brick and slate roof garage on site, break out floor slab, grub out foundations complete, and clear and cart away from site all debris.

4.00   EXCAVATION AND EARTHWORK

4.01   Strip site. Excavate the whole area of the works and pavings average depth 150 mm and wheel and cart away from site to tip.

4.02   Excavate for foundations. Excavate trenches for foundations to the widths and depths indicated on the drawings, return, fill in and ram selected excavated material around footings.

4.03   Excavate for water service pipe. Excavate for new main water service at a depth not less than 750 mm below finished ground level, from water authority's service to stopcock position. Carefully return, fill in over and consolidate over new service pipe.

4.04   Excavate for drainage. Excavate for drain runs, gullies and manholes as shown on the drawings to the required dimensions, levels and falls, grade and consolidate bottoms and return, fill in and consolidate on completion. Break in sides of trenches under pavings to three times the width of the trench before filling in.

4.05   Hardcore. Make up to required levels under concrete beds and pavings with approved brick hardcore broken to pass a 75 mm gauge, levelled, consolidated, blinded with fine material and finished with 500 g Visqueen to receive concrete. Visqueen is to be laid with 150 mm end and side laps and turned up around perimeter above the level of the damp proof course.

A general clause dealing with removal of surplus soil and water removal.

Specify sulphate resisting to BS 4027, 1980 where required in clay subsoils in lieu.

A general clause to cover all aggregates suitable for good concrete work.

Concrete mixes may vary somewhat but those shown are suitable for domestic work. Where more controlled mixes are either required by the construction or specified by the consultant engineer they should be inserted in lieu.

Any testing required should be incorporated in this clause. For cube tests a Provisional Sum should be inserted to cover the cost of testing.

Any steel fabric to be used should be specified to BS 4483: 1969 and the specific BS reference to mesh size indicated for specific situations. Laps should be 150 mm to all sheets and securely wired together and set up on spacers to provide the proper cover to the underside.

Formwork and falsework design is the contractor's responsibility. Striking is the responsibility of the architect or of the consultant engineer if he is employed on supervision.

A general clause for holes and mortises. Specific holes should be so specified, e.g. fixing metal balusters.

4.06   <u>Cart away</u>. Clear and cart away from site to tip all surplus excavated material as it accumulates and keep all excavations clear of water by pumping or baling as required.

5.00   CONCRETE WORK

5.01   <u>Cement.</u> Cement shall be Portland of British manufacture to BS 12: 1978, of normal setting quality, delivered in the manufacturer's sealed bags and stored in dry conditions to prevent deterioration.

5.02   <u>Aggregates</u>. Coarse aggregate for concrete work shall consist of natural gravel, crushed gravel or stone free from all deleterious matter, and fine aggregate shall consist of well-graded, clean, sharp pit or river sand to pass a 4.76 mm sieve, all complying with BS 882, Pt 2: 1973, and of the nominal sizes stated.

5.03   <u>Concrete</u>. Concrete shall be as follows:
Mix A – one part cement to seven parts all-in aggregate to pass a 38 mm sieve
Mix B – one part cement to seven parts all-in aggregate to pass a 19 mm sieve
Mix C – one part cement to two parts fine aggregate to four parts coarse aggregate to pass a 19 mm sieve
Mix D – one part cement to twelve parts all-in aggregate to pass 19 mm sieve

5.04   The concrete shall be prepared in an approved mixer, or delivered to site ready mixed to BS 5328: 1981, with only enough water added to give a good workable mix of uniform colour and consistency and a slump not exceeding 50 mm.

5.05   All concrete shall be placed in position as rapidly as possible by means to prevent segregation and no throwing or dropping will be allowed. No concreting shall be carried out when the temperature is less than $2°C$ and in frosty weather all new concrete shall be properly protected.

5.06   <u>Reinforcement</u>. All mild steel reinforcement shall be free from oil, dirt, loose rust or other deleterious matter. Hot rolled steel bars shall conform to BS 4449: 1978 and mesh to BS 4483: 1969. All reinforcement shall be properly fixed in position before the concrete is placed, all bars to have hooked ends and intersections secured with galvanized steel wire. Reinforcement is to be provided with approved spacers to ensure correct concrete cover.

5.07   <u>Formwork</u>. All formwork is to be solidly and rigidly constructed to safely carry the weight of wet concrete without deflection or leakage. Where a fair face is to be provided the formwork shall be lined with approved hardboard or plywood. Formwork shall not be struck until written authority has been obtained from the architect.

5.08   <u>Form all holes</u>. Form all holes, sinkings, grooves and mortises in concrete, as necessary and required by all trades, as the work proceeds, or cut away for and make good after.

Any reinforcement required should be incorporated together with cover specified. Changes of level should be specified against sawn vertical shutter.

Oversite concrete beds may be specified over cold bitumen or other d.p.m.s laid on to weak concrete blinding. Care should be taken to specify continuity between d.p.c. and d.p.m.

Lintels over 1200 mm generally require a calculation and design sheet to be submitted by a structural engineer. These lintels and their reinforcement may be specified separately or the whole of the lintels specified to suit.

Special labours, details, fixings, etc., should be described for particular lintels in a separate clause, in order to draw attention to them.

Lintels to be fair face should be separately described. Where plastered they may be finished rough or have an application of a bonding agent specified in Floor, wall and ceiling finishes.

5.09   Foundations. Form strip foundations of concrete Mix A of the widths and thickness shown on the drawings, well consolidated and levelled to steel levelling pins to receive brickwork.

5.10   Concrete beds. Provide and lay to whole of ground floor area concrete Mix B 100 mm thick, on layer of Visqueen previously specified, well tamped and consolidated, floated smooth in fuel store and garage and otherwise prepared to receive screeds, the concrete to finish either level with the d.p.c. (if self-finished) or set down below d.p.c. level the full thickness of the screed, whichever is applicable.

5.11   Form bed of concrete Mix A 150 mm deep under paving to rear porch on hardcore previously specified, consolidated and set to fall to receive pavings specified hereafter.

5.12   Form lintels of concrete Mix C to openings of dimensions shown and reinforced as specified. Lintels are to have 150 mm bearing at each end.

Door   D 1   275 × 150 reinf. 2 no. 12 mm m.s. bars
         D 2–6   275 × 150 reinf. 2 no. 9 mm m.s. bars
         D 8   275 × 150 reinf. 2 no. 12 mm m.s. bars
         D 9   100 × 150 reinf. 1 no. 19 mm m.s. bars
         D10   275 × 150 reinf. 2 no. 12 mm m.s. bars
         D11   100 × 150 reinf. 1 no. 9 mm m.s. bars
         D12   275 × 150 reinf. 2 no. 9 mm m.s. bars
         D13–15 100 × 150 reinf. 1 no. 9 mm m.s. bars
         D16   275 × 150 reinf. 2 no. 12 mm m.s. bars
         D17   100 × 150 reinf. 1 no. 9 mm m.s. bars

Window W1   275 × 150 reinf. 2 no. 9 mm m.s. bars
          W2–4   275 × 150 reinf. 2 no. 12 mm m.s. bars
          W5–7   275 × 150 reinf. 2 no. 9 mm m.s. bars
          W8   275 × 150 reinf. 2 no. 12 mm m.s. bars
          W9   275 × 150 reinf. 2 no. 19 mm m.s. bars

5.13   Concrete lintels set behind tile-hanging are to have matching plain tile cast into soffit externally to project 50 mm and to provide tilter over door and window openings.

5.14   All lintels to be finished rough to receive plaster where required. Lintels to windows to be each provided internally with 4 no. hardwood dovetailed fixing blocks to the vertical face for pelmets where directed.

Unless the facing brick is specified to type from a specific brickworks or brick factor, a PC Sum per thousand should be inserted.

Common bricks can be specified as shown or as 'seconds' from stock brick areas.

Care must be taken in specifying blocks that they will meet the requirements of Part FF of the Building Regulations.

The selection of wall tie will depend on its location, the specific requirements of building control, etc. and the appropriate type specified. All metal ties (butterfly, vertical twist and double triangle) are included in BS 1243.

Sulphate resisting cement to BS 4027, 1980 should be specified for mortars below d.p.c. where necessary and used in the concrete foundation mixes. Mortar should be specified for the brick or block location and exposure and to manufacturer's recommendations.

BS 743 covers a range of bitumen d.p.c.s:
Type A   Hessian base
Type B   Fibre base
Type C   Asbestos base
Type D   Hessian base and lead
Type E   Fibre base and lead
Type F   Asbestos base and lead

The specification for external walls will vary with the specific requirements of the Building Regulations, Part F, for example the thickness of the inner block leaf. In addition, the incorporation of additional insulation within the cavity void may be required and this should be incorporated here. This will be specific to the system used and follow the maker's recommendations. Where a subcontractor is to be employed a Prime Cost Sum should be incorporated.

6.00   BRICKWORK AND BLOCKWORK

6.01   <u>Bricks.</u> Facing bricks shall be approved sound, hard, well burnt, truly shaped 65 mm
Hamsey multi-stock facing bricks, free from defects and inclusions, supplied by . . .
and equal to a sample approved by the architect.

6.02   Common bricks below d.p.c. and in manholes shall be approved 65 mm Class B clay
bricks to BS 3921: 1974. Common bricks internally above d.p.c. will be approved 65 mm
calcium silicate common bricks to BS 187: 1978.

6.03   <u>Blocks.</u> The inner leaf of the cavity wall, the backing wall to the tile-hanging and all
internal partitions coloured green on the drawings shall be constructed from approved
cellular lightweight blocks manufactured by . . . and of the thicknesses indicated
on the drawings. The cavity wall to the garage will be faced internally with approved
concrete blocks to BS 6073, Pt 1: 1981.

6.04   <u>Wall ties.</u> Wall ties shall be galvanized wire butterfly pattern to BS 1243: 1978, built in
at intervals of 900 mm horizontally and 450 mm vertically with extra ties at corners
and reveals.

6.05   <u>Mortar.</u> Sand for brickwork shall be clean sharp river or pit sand to BS 1198, 1199,
1200: 1976. Cement shall be Portland to BS 12: 1978 of normal setting quality. Lime
shall be hydrated to BS 890: 1972.

6.06   Cement mortar shall be composed of one part cement to three parts of sand (1:3).
Compo mortar shall be composed of one part cement to one part lime to six parts sand
(1:1:6). Mortar for lightweight insulated blockwork shall be composed of one part
cement to two parts lime to nine parts sand (1:2:9).

6.07   <u>Damp course.</u> The damp course shall be bitumen fibre based to BS 743: 1970 Type B,
the full width of the walls and partitions and 225 mm wide to reveals in cavity walling,
tacked to the backs of the frames, set 12 mm back from the external face of the brick
reveal and set to pass into the cavity. Provide and fix d.p.c.s 100 mm wide to underside
of all timber sills.

6.08   <u>Workmanship.</u> Build the walls to the heights and dimensions shown on the drawings,
the cavity work to comprise an outer skin of brick, 50 mm cavity, an inner skin of brick
up to d.p.c. level and thence in 100 mm block as specified. Facing bricks to commence
one course below finished ground level, and walls to tile-hung areas to be 215 mm solid
block, separated from facing work by a course of plain clay tiles set to project 50 mm
as tilter.

A general clause to cover block partitions and labours.

A clause to cover a specific feature for the exterior of the building.

A clause to cover a specific feature for the interior of the building (see also 11.01).

A general clause to cover sundry labours and items for the Brickwork and blockwork.

Stone is always specified either from a nominated supplier or direct from the quarry specifying the material by name or by bed. The quality of the finish is also necessary: stone to be built against brick or block backing needs to be sawn square, whereas stone built into a stone wall can be rough drafted. The style of walling also needs to be described, e.g. block in course, random rubble, coursed ashlar or snecked rubble.

Mortars vary with stones used. Stone dust should be used sparingly except on fine-jointed work.
Typical mixes are:

lime:sand	1:3 (generally)
cement:lime:sand	1:2:9 (exposed details)
	1:1:6 (for most sandstones)
cement:sand	1:3 (granite)

6.09   Mortars shall be mixed on a clean boarded platform sufficient only for one day's work and no knocking up will be permitted. Pointing shall be carried out as the work proceeds, the joint cut off flush with the trowel and lightly firmed with a soft brush. All brickwork below d.p.c. and above roof level shall be in cement mortar (1:3), the remainder in compo mortar (1:1:6); mortar for blockwork will be 1:1:9.

6.10   Build in wall ties as the work proceeds, keep cavities free from droppings and clear ties and d.p.c.s of all mortar in cavity. Build in all horizontal d.p.c.s to walls, vertical d.p.c.s to reveals, lead trays and flashings and point up on completion. Build in concrete lintels, bedding same on d.p.c. carried vertically at end to provide expansion joint full depth next wall.

6.11   Partitions. All partitions coloured green on the drawings are to be of block as specified, block bonded to brickwork and of the thicknesses shown. Carry out all cutting and fitting required.

6.12   Brick plinth. Form brick plinth to front elevation of facings in cement mortar 1:3 to receive ornamental feature as detail drawings.

6.13   Brick fireplace. Include the Provisional Sum of £ _____ for the construction of brick feature wall and fireplace in lounge complete.

6.14   Attendance. Carry out all cutting, fitting and bonding required; build in all frame ties, fixings, cramps, dowels, plates and frames; attend upon, cut away for and make good after all trades.

7.00   RUBBLE WALLING AND MASONRY

7.01   Stone. Stone for walling shall be . . . obtained from . . . , free from vents, beds, streaks and all other imperfections and prepared for setting in its natural bed. Each stone is to hold to the full size, sawn square at the back, jointed and with roughly dressed face.

7.02   Stone panel. The stone panel shown on the drawings is to be built in uncoursed snecked rubble roughly dressed square laid with all horizontal joints, the maximum height not exceeding 250 mm and of snecks 75 mm.

7.03   Mortar. The mortar for bedding and jointing the rubble panel will be one part cement to three parts lime putty to twelve parts sand (for limestones and porous sandstones only), the quantities gauged by volume, and properly mixed in an approved mixer. Only sufficient water shall be added to provide a workable mix. Mortar joints will be finished as the work proceeds with the bedding joint left slightly protruding and cleaned off slightly recessed pointed on completion.

Asphalt is a rigid material and care must be taken to prevent adhesion at angles where movement in the supporting structure can exert stress, i.e. dressing over timber-splayed fillets at junction between walls and roofs. Vertical surfaces must be well keyed and primed or provided with expanded metal to form support and key.

A wearing deck of asbestos tiles bedded in a bitumen bonding coat can be specified for foot traffic.

Concrete tiles should be specified to BS 473 and 550, Pt 2: 1971, and the type and manufacturer's name should be included.

The gauge and batten sizes should be varied for the particular tile used.

Single lap tiles have different eaves, verge and hip specifications and should be described for the tile selected.

Ridges vary with tile used and should match manufacturer's recommendations.

Single lap tiles usually have no soakers and stack or abutment flashing dressed over the 'roll' to seal the abutment junction.

7.04   Clean down the face of the stonework as scaffold is removed to produce a perfect finish and cover up and protect the work by approved means from frost or heavy rain.

8.00   ASPHALT WORKS

8.01   Asphalt shall comply with BS 1162, 1410, 1418: 1973 and the whole of the work will be carried out by an approved specialist subcontractor strictly to CP 144, Pt 4: 1970.

8.02   Lay to roof of garage and dormer window on and including a layer of approved black sheathing felt to BS 747: 1977, asphalt in three coats to a total thickness of 28 mm, with minimum laps of 150 mm and the final layer proper finished by rubbing with sharp sand. The asphalt to the dormer shall be carried up lier board and dressed over the tilter, and the open edges of both roofs shall be finished with a solid water check roll and 100 mm deep apron with undercut drip at bottom edge.

8.03   Properly make good asphalt flat around rainwater outlet, dress asphalt into luting flanges and leave all perfect and watertight on completion.

9.00   ROOFING

9.01   Roof tiling. The whole of the pitched roofs shall be covered with sound, well burnt cambered antique machine-made, sand-faced plain clay tiles to BS 402, 1979. Tiles and fittings to be supplied by . . . and equal to a sample to be deposited with and approved by the architect.

9.02   The tiles are to be laid to a 100 mm gauge on 39 x 19 sawn softwood battens to BS 4471, Pt 2: 1971, treated with water-borne preservative compositions to BS 4072: 1974, over approved untearable foil-backed sarking felt to BS 747: 1977 Type 1F, the latter fixed with 150 mm laps and dressed over the fascia into the gutters.

9.03   The tiles are to have a double course at eaves and tile, and a half course at verges with undercloak, sunk pointed in cement mortar (1:3). All hips are to be finished with proper matching bonnet hip tiles bedded and flush-pointed in cement mortar (1:3). All tiling is to be nailed at eaves, verges, hips and every fifth course using non-ferrous nails.

9.04   Cover the ridges with matching hog-back clay ridge tiles, bedded and pointed in cement mortar (1:3), free ends neatly and fully filled in with tile slips.

9.05   Carry out all necessary cutting and fitting and making out with tile and half as required, inserting lead soakers provided to all abutments, one to each tile. Remove all damaged or defective tiles and replace with new, clear out gutters and leave roof perfect and water-tight on completion.

Tile-hanging in clay and in concrete tiles are identical in principle. The type of tile selected and its pattern (plain, club, arrow, beavertail, etc.) should conform to relevant BS. Special angle tiles should be specified for internal and external angles. Abutments between tiles and brick returns can be provided with a vertical lead Code 4 stepped flashing dressed behind the tile hanging 150 mm (see also 9.13).

Screws where required for fixings, e.g. lead dots, should be brass or stainless steel to BS 1210: 1963. Solder should be Grade D or J to BS 219: 1959.

The underlay can also be waterproof building paper to BS 1521: 1972 Class A where plywood or similar forms the decking. For uneven or boarded decking, felt as specified is best.

An alternative is super purity aluminium to BS 1470: 1972 Gauge 6; zinc to BS 849: 1939. The application of a coat of bitumen paint to BS 3416: 1975 Type 1 is used on all metals in contact with mortars.

A general clause which covers the abutment of all vertical wall surfaces to raking tiled and slated roof slopes.

Where a particular species of timber is required for decorative or other reasons, it must be specified. Samples for approval should be sought.

9.06   Tile-hanging. Provide to areas shown on the drawings sound, well-burnt, red machine-made, sand-faced plain clay tiles to BS 402, 1979. Tiles and fittings to be supplied by . . . and equal to a sample to be deposited with an approved by the architect.

9.07   Hang the tiles on 38 × 19 sawn softwood battens as specified before fixed to 112 mm gauge through waterproof building paper to BS 1521: 1972 Type A2F to block walling. Each tile is to be fixed with 2 no. non-ferrous nails to battens, with double course of tiles at eaves and proper angle tiles, except to dormers where free end of tiled cheeks are to project 25 mm proud of window frame and neatly sunk-pointed in cement and sand (1:3). Abutments of tile-hanging and raking slope of gable roof to be Winchester cut. Neatly cut tiles around lead-covered fixing blocks for r.w.p.s.

9.08   Finish the eaves to garage with two courses of tile hanging weathered with asphalt apron as described before.

9.09   Leadwork. Sheet lead shall be best English milled to BS 1178, 1982, uniform in thickness, free from cracks and defects and to the thickness specified.

9.10   Workmanship shall be to CP 143, Pt 11: 1970, the lead well and neatly dressed without injury to the surface and provision made for expansion and contraction without injury. All nailing is to be carried out using copper nails. Paint all lead in contact with mortar one coat bitumen paint to BS 3416: 1975 Type 1 before building in.

9.11   Lead flat. Provide and lay to roof of oriel window brown sheathing felt No. 1 Type 4B (ii) to BS 747, 1977 with 50 x 45 tapered and rounded softwood rolls at 600 mm centres. Lay to roof Code 5 sheet lead all to CP 143, dress lead 150 mm vertically behind tile-hanging and form neat welted drip to front edge secured with lead tacks at 600 mm centres.

9.12   Leadwork to chimney. Provide and fix Code 4 lead safe to chimney perforated for flue and turned up around perforation 25 mm. Provide and fix Code 4 lead soakers, cover flashing, saddle and apron as required and shown on drawings.

9.13   Leadwork to dormer windows. Provide and fix Code 4 lead soakers to junction of vertical tiling and roof slopes, one soaker to each tile. Provide and fix to underside of sill to bathroom window Code 4 lead cover flashing, neatly dressed 150 mm down over tiling with decorative cut to bottom edge.

10.00   WOODWORK

10.01   Timber. Timber for carcassing shall be selected from species complying with the requirements of CP 112 softwood Group II with measurement characteristics affecting strength in accordance with BS 4978: 1973.

Where joinery is to be left natural finish this should be so stated so that a clear preservative fluid treatment for the timber can be selected.

The moisture content of timber can be specified to BS 1186, Pt 1: 1971.

The particular sizes of roof timbers should be inserted together with details of all connectors, special straps and bolts to be employed. Where trussed rafters are to be used the BS and the name and address of supplier should be inserted together with any special requirements for roof access, trimming, etc. It is advisable to also insert requirements for preservative treatment and type of weathering material specified.

Any special fixings to hold down the timbers should be added together with fixing centres and method of securing. The name of the manufacturer and list numbers, centres of fixing and finish should also be incorporated.

Any fixings required for loft ladders should be added here. If necessary the loft ladder should be specified out or a PC Sum included.

If a stillage is required to raise the head it should be incorporated here.

10.02   Timber for joinery shall be 'unsorted' grade and of approved species selected from and conforming to BS 1186, Pt 1: 1971 and prepared to conform to BS 4471, Pt 1: 1978.

10.03   Softwood for carcassing and joinery shall be treated with water-borne copper/chrome/arsenic compositions to BS 4072: 1974.

10.04   The contractor is responsible for ensuring that the moisture content of timber used is appropriate to the situation and conditions in which the material is to be employed.

10.05   Roof framing. The whole of the pitched roofs shall be constructed to comply with CP 112, Pt 2: 1971 and as shown on the drawings to a pitch of 50 degrees and of timber sizes as follows:

Rafters, ceiling joists, purlin struts and binders }	100 × 50 at 400 mm centres
Purlins	175 × 50
Hangers	75 × 50
Hip and valley rafters	200 × 38
Dormer rafters	75 × 38 at 400 mm centres
Ridgeboard	175 × 25
Wall plates	100 × 75

The work will be cut, fitted and put together in a sound and workmanlike manner, properly framed up, jointed, spiked and bolted as required.

10.06   Flat roof decking. Form the flat roofs to the bathroom, utility room and garage as shown on the drawings and as follows:

Joists to bathroom dormer, 100 × 38 at 400 mm centres
Joists to utility room and garage, 225 × 38 at 600 mm centres

Provide and fix to midspan of roofs to utility room and garage 50 × 38 sawn softwood herringbone strutting.
Provide and lay to flat roof areas Purldek incorporating 6.5 mm ply for asphalt secured, fixed and free edges supported on 50 × 38 sawn softwood nogging all in accordance with the manufacturer's instructions. All sheets should be slightly gapped and fixed with 50 mm 12 s.w.g. ring shank nails at 100 mm centres to perimeter and 300 mm centres elsewhere. Form openings and trim round for r.w.p.s, S & VPs and flue.

10.07   Roof access. Provide and fix trimmers and form openings where shown on the drawings for 2 no. roof access hatches, each size 900 × 600 clear. Form hatch with 25 mm prepared softwood lining and 25 × 19 planted stops with standard architrave moulding on underside. Provide and lay in position 12 mm blockboard to BS 3444: 1972 with edges lipped as loose cover.

10.08   Tank support. Provide and spike to ceiling joists in roof space 3 no. 100 × 50 sawn softwood bearers with 25 mm p.t. & g. boarded platform as support for cold-water cistern.

An alternative is to use resin-bonded flooring-grade chipboard (see 10.14).

Soffit can be in p.t. & g. softwood vee-jointed boarding.

Where joists are carried on external walls the use of joist hangers can be specified here. Also, where joists are carried from both sides on to half brick or 100 mm block walls the use of saddle-type double hangers can be specified.

Deal-painted aprons can be specified here.

Nogging is required to support all free edges of chipboard flooring.

Skirtings can be described to suit details or to BS 584: 1967.

See above for skirtings.

This applies to trim which is to be polished or otherwise finished clear.

In high-class work two coats of knotting and priming are usual, at least on all bedding faces for priming.

Alternatively, where painted or in cheaper work, linings can be 25 mm with 38 x 19 planted softwood stops; *or*, door sets from a specified manufacturer can be used.

10.09   Roof boarding. Provide and lay in roof space and spike down to ceiling joists 6 metres square 19 mm p.t. & g. softwood flooring.

10.10   Fascia and soffit. Form eaves with 100 x 25 prepared softwood fascia grooved at back to receive 6 mm WBP grade plywood soffit to BS 1455: 1972, complete with 50 x 25 sawn softwood bearers at 400 centres and all prepared for painting.

10.11   Lier board. Provide and securely spike to jack rafters at junction of flat and pitched roofs 25 mm prepared softwood square-edge boarding complete with 38 x 75 splayed tilter.

10.12   First floor construction. Form and construct the first floor with 225 x 38 sawn softwood joists at 400 mm centres, with double joists under main spine partition. Provide 225 x 75 trimmers to stairwell and chimney breast properly tusk-tenoned to trimmers. Provide and securely spike to joists 2 no. rows of 50 x 38 sawn softwood herringbone strutting to floors of both bedrooms and study.

10.13   Provide and secret fix to trimmed opening to stairwell 25 mm prepared Columbian pine apron with plaster groove and rounded free edge, tongued to and including 100 x 25 prepared margin to match.

10.14   Provide and fix as required, 50 x 38 sawn softwood nogging between joists to give support as recommended to all free edges, provide and lay to the whole of the first floor 19 mm rebated-edge resin-bonded, flooring-grade wood chipboard to BS 5669: 1979, securely nailed at 150 mm centres to manufacturer's recommendations, nail heads well punched home. Include for all cutting and waste.

10.15   Skirtings. Provide and fix to perimeter of all rooms except bathrooms, kitchen, fuel store and garage 75 x 19 prepared and moulded Columbian pine skirting with neatly scribed internal angles and properly finished tight to architraves.

10.16   Architraves. Provide and fix to both sides of all internal doors 75 x 25 prepared and moulded Columbian pine architraves with neatly mitred external angles.

10.17   The bedding faces *only* of all architraves, skirtings and internal door linings are to be primed with approved aluminium primer sealer before fixing.

10.18   Building in. Door and window frames are to be built in as the work proceeds and all faces are to be knotted and primed before being fixed. Provide, screw to backs of frames and build into brick or block courses, at intervals not exceeding 675 mm vertically, approved sheradized pressed steel fixing cramps.

10.19   Internal door linings. All internal door linings are to be 38 mm prepared, rebated and rounded Columbian pine, tongued at angles and fixed with 6 no. sheradized steel cramps to each jamb.

Doors are generally stock from a specialist manufacturer. Specials should always be specified separately and full details given.

Alternatively for painted doors pressed steel or nylon hinges are used, one pair for lightweight hardboard or ply-faced doors.

The sill detail is important to stop water penetration. Galvanized wrot iron water bars or patent aluminium sill sections can be used and should be specified accordingly. Water bars are set in grooves and run in either in lead or neat cement grout.

External doors may be standard stock or specials depending on the designer's requirements. Glass can be puttied in or fixed either with pinned beads or beads with brass sockets and screws. Weatherboards may be hardwood and can be let into the frame at either side to provide a more weatherproof seal.

Special doors and frames should be fully specified, with special care taken with the labours.

The internal lining to door D10 is to be 32 mm ditto plain, not rebated, and split to suit sliding door installation.

10.20   <u>Internal doors</u>. Internal doors shall be Type B solid core flush doors generally to BS 459, Pt 2: 1962 manufactured by . . . and faced with . . . and, except where specified hereafter, prepared for painting. All doors will hold to size 1981 x 762 x 38 finished thickness except Door D14 which will hold to size 1981 x 610 x 38.

10.21   The following doors shall be finished to special order both (2) sides or one (1) side only with 6 mm <u>Columbian pine</u> faced plywood generally to BS 1455: 1972 Type INT to approved sample with superfine finish:
D 9 (2)
D10 (2)
D11 (1)
D13 (1)
D14 (1)
D15 (1)
D16 (2)
D17 (1)

10.22   Each internal door shall be hung on 1½ pairs of 75 mm brass, washered hinges to BS 1227, Pt 1A: 1967 Table 23 and the bottoms of doors shot in after carpets fitted to the approval of the architect.

10.23   <u>External door frames</u>. External door frames generally shall be 100 x 65 prepared, twice rebated and rounded softwood with 150 x 75 rebated, weathered and throated <u>utile</u> sill, all securely framed with mortise and tenon joints secured with hardwood dowels and prepared for painting. Frames for doors D3, D4 and D5 will be supplied without sills, the ends of the posts being provided with Code 4 lead perforated for and the frames secured to concrete with 9 mm mild steel dowels 150 mm long.

10.24   <u>External doors</u>. External doors generally shall be 1981 x 838 x 50 softwood nominal thickness to BS 459, Pt 1: 1954 open and divided into 10 no. lights complete with glazing bars and all prepared for and including glazing beads and prepared for painting. Doors shall be provided with 75 x 65 prepared splayed, moulded and grooved softwood weatherboard bedded in white lead and secured through the door with long steel screws with their heads let in and pelleted from the inside.

10.25   Doors D3, D4 and D5 shall be 1981 x 762 x 50 nominal thickness ledged, framed, braced and battened softwood doors generally to BS 459, Pt 4: 1965 and prepared for painting.

10.26   Each external door shall be hung on 1½ pairs 100 mm cast iron butt hinges to BS 1227, Pt 1A: 1967 Table 18.

10.27   <u>Front entrance door and frame</u>, all to be in selected and approved <u>English oak</u>. Construct

Hardwood doors should always be hung on b.m.a. or brass hinges left with natural finish. The preparation of the timbers for their final finish should be specified, for example for liming, varnish or french polish (the latter for internal use only), etc.

Garage doors, operating gear and track are to be specified, along with the manufacturer, the pattern or type of door, its size and finish or material. Any framing or linings required around the opening, and special labours for glazing or glass, should be included.

The appropriate BS for the type of window should be incorporated, along with the name of the manufacturer. Any special items such as surrounds, sills, mullions and transomes shall be specified and a schedule of windows with references to manufacturer or BS types should be added. Any special requirements for double-glazing units, gasket seals and primers should be incorporated.

Special windows should be fully specified in accordance with the architect's wishes.

Window boards should be specified to material, for example quarry tile, softwood, hardwood or glazed tiles, together with any special finish to free edge, etc. All timber boards must be back primed (softwood) or sealed (hardwood) before fixing; hardwood should have pelleted screw fixings.

Kitchen and other fittings are covered by Provisional or Prime Cost Sums (see Chapter 3).

the frame with 100 x 65 twice rebated and rounded head and posts and 150 x 65 twice rebated, weathered and throated sill, the fixed sidelight complete with 25 x 15 Oak beads with brass sockets and screws. Hang to frame on 1½ pairs 100 mm b.m.a. finish butt hinges with steel pins and washers, 838 x 1981 x 50 nominal thickness Oak ledged, framed, braced and battened door, moulded bead and butt to detail. Prepare opening in centre ledge and battens for letter plate and prepare door and frame for liming.

10.28   Garage doors. Provide and fix to opening 100 x 65 prepared and rebated softwood frame and transome open and divided into four lights for putty glazing and with 100 x 100 prepared softwood centre post to floor to receive door gear and complete with lead d.p.c. and m.s. dowels to bottom of posts to concrete as before described. Provide and fix to openings 2 no. . . . up and over garage doors, each size . . ., including providing fixings to ceiling over to receive horizontal track as manufacturer's fixing instructions.

10.29   Windows. Windows shall be M4 hot dip galvanized steel units to BS 990, Pt 2: 1972 manufactured by . . . and fixed in accordance with the manufacturer's instructions to prepared softwood frames to BS 1285: 1980 incorporating sills Type 2. The following windows are required:

9C2	16 no.
9F2	3 no.
9FV2	9 no.
7F2	2 no.
7C2	1 no.
11CV2	2 no.
11F2	2 no.

All metal windows are to be prepared for double glazing units and all faces primed with plumbate primer before fixing.

10.30   Construct the oriel window generally as specified before and carried on 75 x 50 sawn softwood bearers set flat and well secured down to top of wall, complete with 75 x 19 prepared softwood skirt rebated for and including 6 mm WBP-grade plywood soffit to BS 1455: 1972. Provide and build into wall 2 no. 200 x 50 prepared and moulded softwood brackets 725 mm long to detail. Form canopy over with bearers and fascia and complete with 6 mm ply deck, all as described before, and prepare for lead.

10.31   Window boards. Provide and fix to all ground floor windows *except* kitchen, cloakroom and bathrooms, 25 mm prepared Columbian pine window boards, cross-tongued to oriel with sunk moulded nosings, neatly cut in and returned between reveals. The boards are to be back primed before fixing, as described before, and sealed before plastering.

10.32   Wardrobe fitting. Include the Provisional Sum of £＿＿＿＿ for wardrobe fitting in bedroom no. 1.

10.33   Kitchen fittings. Include the PC Sum of £＿＿＿＿ for the supply and delivery to site of . . . kitchen fittings by a supplier to be nominated by the architect.

Shelving to linen cupboards is usually batten type with spacers for the air to circulate, while solid shelving (cross tongued over 200 mm wide) is used for cupboards and larders.

Roof insulation and vapour barriers should be described for each particular circumstance.

Tanks in roof space require covers and insulation to suit.

Framing is required to some bath panels to suit.

Specify fully for staircases except where stock stairs are to be used as manufactured and selected from a catalogue. Special stairs include balusters, newels and handrails. Details of apron and trim to stairwell should also be incorporated.

Ironmongery either can be the subject of a Prime Cost Sum or each item can be selected with number and maker's reference and scheduled in the specification. If a PC Sum is used quantities of each item should be incorporated to allow the estimator to price accurately for fixing.

Structural steelwork is described in a separate trade heading immediately before Metal-

Add for profit, taking delivery, moving to position and fixing complete the following units:

1 no. sink unit complete with stainless steel single drainer top size 1200 x 600
3 no. 1200 x 600 cupboard units each with 2 no. drawers and complete with worktops
4 no. 1200 x 600 x 300 deep wall units

10.34   Batten shelving. Provide and fix in linen cupboard 6 no. 50 x 25 prepared softwood slatted shelves on ditto bearers plugged and screwed to walls, the shelves to be full width and depth of cupboard and all removable.

10.35   Roof insulation. Provide and lay over or incorporate in all sloping and flat ceiling slopes and to side cheeks of dormers . . . mm . . . insulation.

10.36   Tank insulation. Provide and fix 25 mm polystyrene tank lagging set to cold water storage cistern complete with cover. Carry out all cutting and fitting required and securely wire on.

10.37   Bath panels. Provide and fix sawn softwood framing to receive bath panels.

10.38   Staircase. Provide and securely fix to trimmers new staircase of Columbian pine in single flight with 25 mm treads and 19 mm risers all tongued together and fixed with steel screws, nosing slightly rounded and with small scotia under, wedged and blocked to 38 mm prepared Columbian pine strings, and rebated for plaster as required. Provide and fix prepared softwood bearers to soffit and prepare for plasterboard and set finish. Provide and fix 100 x 100 prepared pine newels to stair and open well end with moulded capping to detail, 25 x 25 square pine balusters and 75 x 65 prepared moulded pine handrail to well and open side of staircase and prepare all for sealing and waxing.

10.39   Ironmongery. Include the PC Sum of £   for the supply and delivery to site of ironmongery, patterns to be as selected and directed by the architect. Add for profit, sorting and fixing as follows:

23 no.   latch sets and mortise locks complete with knob handles
 4 no.   rim night latches
 1 no.   letter plate
 6 no.   mortise bolts

Ironmongery is to be fixed with matching screws, removed for background painting and refixed on completion. All locks shall be lightly oiled and adjusted on completion of the works.

11.00   METALWORK

11.01   Arch bar. Provide and build into brickwork over fire opening 75 x 6 mm wrot iron flat

work. This section incorporates metal windows; as they are required in wooden frames, they have been incorporated for supply and fixing in Woodwork.

All small items of metalwork and the particular protection against corrosion are included in this trade section.

Metal doors and windows, wrot iron gates, brackets and miscellaneous metal fittings are to be specified here.

The particular material and type of gutter, the maker and all fittings and fixings should be specified.

Rainwater pipes are generally from the same maker as gutters. Any specials, e.g. offsets, and fittings, such as shoes, should be described. Special fixings required to facing materials should be specified.

Soil and vent shafts are generally specified to the appropriate BS and the maker's name may be added. Fixing, jointing and all branches should be carefully specified.

Some S & VPs incorporate a special guard at the head which should be used, e.g. uPVC.

A general clause to cover statutory requirements.

Service connections are covered by Provisional Sums. As these are net, allowance must be made for contractor's cash discount.

Water service pipes should be sized to suit storage and water board requirements.

A general clause to cover normal copper pipework for domestic plumbing.

arch bar. The metal is to be treated with Jenolite and painted two coats Manders black before fixing.

11.02   Matwell frames. Provide, set in position and run in with neat cement grout 2 no. matwell frames size 750 x 500 x 25 deep (provisional) fabricated from 32 x 6 mm wrot iron flat bar with 6 no. fixing lugs welded on, the whole treated and cleaned down, free from rust and zinc-sprayed after manufacture.

12.00   PLUMBING AND MECHANICAL ENGINEERING SERVICES

12.01   Gutters. Provide and fix where shown on the roof drawings 100 mm half round grey uPVC gutters to BS 4576, Pt 1: 1970 manufactured by . . . complete with all necessary fittings, stop ends and outlets, and fixed in accordance with the manufacturer's instructions.

12.02   Rainwater pipes. Provide and fix in positions indicated on the drawings 75 mm grey uPVC rainwater pipes to BS as above, complete with swan necks, and joint to drain socket at foot with asbestos caulking compound. Provide and fix to brick and blockwork behind with tile-hanging 225 x 75 x 50 hardwood spacers to receive fixing clips, the blocks set into the tile-hanging to be covered with Code 4 lead dressed neatly down over the tiles below.

12.03   Soil and vent shafts. The soil and vent shaft shall be 100 mm cast iron pipe and fittings to BS 416: 1973 properly jointed to drain at foot and caulked with asbestos caulking compound; otherwise joints shall be made and run in lead, set above roof level to heights shown and complete with Code 4 lead soaker flange and tail soldered on and dressed to tiled surface. Provide and fix to suit 1 no. 100 mm WC pan branch incorporating 1 no. 38 mm boss for bath and 32 mm boss for basin waste.

12.04   Wire balloon guards. Provide and fix to heads of r.w.p.s and soil and vent shaft galvanized wire balloon guards.

12.05   Internal plumbing. All internal plumbing shall be carried out to the requirements of the local water authority and the Building Regulations.

12.06   Service connections. Include the Provisional Sum of £   for water and gas service connections by statutory undertakings. Add 2½% to the value of the Provisional Sum to cover for loss of discount.

12.07   Water service. Provide and run 15 mm copper service pipe, as specified later, wrapped in Denso tape from service pipe to terminate in a brass screw down combined stop and drain cock, to BS 1010, Pt 2: 1973.

12.08   Pipework. All pipework will be copper to BS 2871, Pt 2: 1972 and jointed with approved

A general clause to cover domestic copper rising main to ball valve of storage cistern. A hose union supply has been added here.

Storage cistern should be specified to suit material selected as to makers or BS type and size. Overflow pipe diameter is always one pipe size larger than supply.

The size of service pipes will depend on the flow required. For single bathroom/cloakroom/kitchen installations 22 mm service to bath with 15 mm to WC and basins will be sufficient. Separate service, usually 28 mm, is required to the boiler.

The size of the cylinder will depend on consumption. For single bathroom dwellings a BS Ref. 8 132-litre cylinder would be sufficient.

The size of the service for a single bathroom dwelling is 22 mm the vent size remaining at 15 mm.

Pipe lagging to be specified to architect's requirements and Building Regulations.

Drying out premises requires a Provisional Sum for fuel cost and attendance.

Nominated subcontracts for heating installations are covered by a Prime Cost Sum.

Builder's work is covered either by a Provisional Sum or by the inclusion of provisional quantities.

Sanitary fittings are the subject of a PC Sum to cover supply by a nominated supplier.

copper-alloy compression fittings. Stop valves will be copper alloy to BS 5154: 1974.

12.09   Main water service. Connect to stopcock and run 15 mm service into roof space and connect to ball valve. Make connection and run 15 mm service to kitchen sink. Make connection with isolating stopcock and run 15 mm supply through external wall where shown to hose union bibcock situated to discharge over kitchen gully.

12.10   Storage cistern. Provide and fix in roof space 1 no. 472-litre asbestos cement cold-water storage cistern to BS 2777: 1974, complete with nylon diaphragm-pattern ball valve to BS 1212, Pt 2: 1970 and plastic float to BS 2456: 1973. Cut away for and make all connections and run 22 mm copper overflow to discharge to open air.

12.11   Cold water service. From storage cistern run 28 mm copper service into second bathroom with 22 mm branch to bath and 15 mm to basin and WC. Continue service in 22 mm pipe into principal bathroom and connect to bath with 15 mm supplies to basin and WC in both bathroom and cloakroom. Provide isolating valve on supply next cistern and on branches to bath, second bathroom and cloakroom.

12.12   From storage cistern run 28 mm supply to hot water cylinder in linen cupboard with isolating valve in cupboard.

12.13   Hot water cylinder. Provide and fix in cylinder cupboard on softwood bearers a BS Ref. 9 152-litre copper indirect cylinder to BS 1566, Pt 2: 1972 complete with boss for immersion heater and 80 mm Heatsaver insulation jacket, and make all connections.

12.14   Hot water service. From top of cylinder take 28 mm pipe with 15 mm vent turned over cistern and run service into second bathroom with 22 mm branch to serve bath and 15 mm to basin. Continue 22 mm service into principal bathroom and connect to bath with 15 mm services to basin, kitchen sink and cloakroom basin. Provide isolating valves on service in linen cupboard, branch service to second bathroom and to cloakroom.

12.15   Lagging. Provide and lag all pipes in roof spaces, duct and floor voids with approved 'Super Foamflex' lagging securely wired on.

12.16   Drying out premises. Include the Provisional Sum of £_____ for fuel for drying out the premises.

12.17   Heating installation. Include the Prime Cost Sum of £_____ for the supply and fixing complete of a gas fired central heating installation by a specialist subcontractor to be nominated by the architect. Add for profit and attendance.

12.18   Builder's work. Include the Provisional Sum of £_____ for builder's work in connection with the heating installation.

12.19   Sanitary fittings. Include the PC Sum of £_____ for the supply and delivery to site of

The number and brief description of the fittings should be incorporated to enable the estimator to price for fixing and connections.

Overflows are always one pipe size larger than service pipes. Flaps can be specified or the free ends splay cut.

Traps and wastes will be specified to suit circumstances and the material to be used. Traps to one-pipe stacks must be deep seal, and waste runs longer than permitted by CP 304 must be provided with anti-vac. pipe or Dirgo automatic air valve.

The size of traps and wastes must be specified to suit the outlet of the fitting.

The electrical installlation is generally covered by the inclusion of a Prime Cost Sum. To enable the estimator to include a sum sufficient to cover attendance, a schedule of points and equipment should be added. In most cases, the electrical contractor will include for chasing, drilling joists, etc. If the contractor is required to carry out this work, the specification should include for this labour.

sanitary fittings by a supplier nominated by the architect as follows:

1 no.   1700 x 700 x 530 p.e. c.i. bath complete with side panel
1 no.   1900 x 800 x 600 p.e. c.i. bath complete with side panel
3 no.   lavatory basins complete with pedestals
3 no.   low level coupled syphonic WC suites complete

Add for profit, unloading, storing, moving to position and fixing complete, including making all connections.

12.20   <u>Overflows</u>. Provide and fix 22 mm copper overflows to WC cisterns set to discharge to open air.

12.21   <u>Traps and wastes</u>. Wastes will be copper tube, as described before, and traps will be copper alloy to BS 1184: 1976 complete with compression fittings. All wastes will be run internally and, where discharging into gullies, brought internally to a position directly above the d.p.c. before penetrating the wall immediately over the gully.

12.22   Provide and install traps and wastes as follows and connect either to bosses on S & VP or set to discharge to gullies as required:

Cloakroom basin ⎫
Principal bathroom basin ⎬   32 mm with 38 mm seal
Kitchen sink   38 mm with 38 mm seal
Principal bath (with overflow connection)   38 mm with 38 mm seal
Secondary bath (with overflow connection)   38 mm with 75 mm seal
Second basin   32 mm with 75 mm seal

12.23   <u>Testing</u>. Include for cutting away for all holes and chases making good. Test the whole of the installation to the reasonable satisfaction of the architect and leave perfect on completion.

13.00   ELECTRICAL INSTALLATION

13.01   <u>Installation</u>. Include the Prime Cost Sum of £_____ for the electrical installation complete, the work to be carried out by a specialist subcontractor to be nominated by the architect. Add for profit and attendance on the following:

18 no. ceiling lighting points
 4 no. wall lighting points
16 no. 13 A twin power points
TV aeriel installation
Cooker control
Bell installation

13.02   <u>Builder's work</u>. All cutting away and chasing shall be carried out by the electrical sub-

Most electrical subcontractors are required to include in their tenders for the main intake cable. The duct is the responsibility of the main contractor and should be specified out for him to price.

General clauses covering the storage and handling of plastering materials. The qualities of basic materials should be amended to meet specific requirements.

A general clause to cover workmanship of the wet plastering trade.

Plaster lath should be 12.7 mm thick where supporting joists are spaced over 400 mm apart and up to 600 mm maximum.

Gyproc cove is supplied in two sizes, 100 and 127 mm girth.

Two-coat plastering is general but three coats are used for high-quality work or where the surface is too uneven and requires dubbing out.

Wall tiles are generally covered by the inclusion of a Prime Cost Sum. The area of tiling contemplated should be given to allow the estimator to make deductions for decorations and to assess attendance.

Floor screeds should be laid in areas not exceeding 15 m^2 where large areas are required. Generally, in domestic work, rooms are small enough to reduce problems of shrinkage. Where subfloors are old or smooth a bonding agent should be specified.

contractor, and the cost of this work is to be included in his subcontract estimate.

13.03   Form main service cable entry duct through the foundations, terminating under the main fuseboard situated in the utility room, the duct to be constructed from 2 no. 100 mm diameter s.g.s. easy bends terminating level with the top surface of the oversite concrete and cased in concrete Mix A.

14.00   FLOOR, WALL AND CEILING FINISHES

14.01   <u>Materials</u>. Materials for wall and ceiling plastering shall be stored in a dry clean place after delivery to site and used in strict rotation.

14.02   Cement and sand shall conform to standards previously specified. Plasterboard lath shall conform to BS 1230: 1970 and gypsum plaster to BS 1191, Pt 1: 1973.

14.03   <u>Workmanship</u>. Internal plastering shall be carried out generally to BS 5492: 1977 and to the manufacturer's particular recommendations. All walls and ceilings are to be finished straight and smooth and to be left free from rough areas, blow holes, dents and other defects, and perfect on completion.

14.04   <u>Ceilings</u>. Line the whole of the ceilings with 9.5 mm foil-backed Gyproc lath, scrim junction of walls and ceilings with 85 mm plasterer's scrim and set in neat Thistle board finish 5 mm thick.

14.05   Provide and fix to perimeter of ceilings in lounge and dining room 100 mm Gyproc cove to manufacturer's instructions.

14.06   <u>Walls</u>. Prepare, float all walls and lintels internally with Thistle browning, rule to even surface, scratch to form a key and finish with 2 mm thick neat Thistle finish. All arrises are to be slightly rounded.

14.07   <u>Wall tiles</u>. Include the Prime Cost Sum of £_____ for the supply and fixing complete of wall tiles to the kitchen, cloakroom and bathroom by a specialist subcontractor to be nominated by the architect. The tiles will be fixed with approved adhesive on to the plastered surface of the walls. Add for profit and attendance on . . . square metres of wall tiling (Provisional).

14.08   <u>Floor screeds</u>. Lay over the whole of the ground floor area EXCEPT to fuel store and garage 1:3 cement and sand screed, well tamped, levelled and consolidated to receive pavings and of the following thicknesses:

Kitchen, cloakroom, bathroom	55 mm
Entrance hall	40 mm
Lounge, dining room and bedroom	60 mm

Floor finishes may be covered by the insertion of a Prime Cost Sum or may be specified out for the builder to make his own arrangements. If the latter, precise directions regarding size, thickness, quality and/or colour should be provided together with the name and address of the makers or suppliers.

A general clause covering the patterns, thickness and characteristics of single- and double-glazed panels.

Metal-glazing compound should be specified against a maker's material, e.g. Berger Mastic GP.

Double-glazed lights can be obtained with both sheets clear or with one clear and one translucent sheet, if a degree of obscuration is required.

Glass to doors can be bedded in a number of materials: washleather and mastic externally, black velvet ribbon internally. Pinned beads are not satisfactory and should be avoided in all except very cheap work. Beads should always be internal to protect them from the weather.

14.09   Check all screeds before completion and hack up and relay any loose or hollow areas.

14.10   Vinyl floor tiling. Include the Prime Cost Sum of £   for the supply and fixing complete of 3.5 mm . . . vinyl tile flooring to kitchen, cloakroom and bathroom by a specialist subcontractor to be nominated by the architect. Add for profit and attendance on . . . square metres of flooring (Provisional).

14.11   Wood block flooring. Include the Prime Cost Sum of £   for the supply and fixing complete of 19 mm . . . wood block flooring to the entrance hall by a specialist sub-contractor to be nominated by the architect. Add for profit and attendance on . . . square metres of flooring (Provisional).

14.12   Cover up and protect all flooring and pavings and leave clean and perfect on completion.

15.00   GLAZING

15.01   Materials. All glass is to be the best of its respective kind complying generally with BS 952, Pt 1: 1978 and BS 5713: 1979 where applicable.

15.02   Linseed oil putty for glazing to wood shall conform to BS 544: 1969 and metal-glazing compound shall be . . . and used strictly in accordance to the manufacturer's recommendations.

15.03   Workmanship. Glazing shall generally be to BS 6262: 1982, the rebates painted with an extra coat of primer as specified hereafter before glazing is commenced.

15.04   Double glazing units. Glaze the whole of the metal windows and external glazed doors and wing lights with hermetically sealed flat double-glazing units to BS 5713: 1979, obtained from an approved manufacturer and fixed strictly to his recommendations. The glass generally will be clear sheet on both faces. The following lights will be glazed internally with narrow Reedlyte translucent glass:
Cloakroom   W5
Bathrooms   W6, W12

15.05   Translucent glass. Glaze the following in Group 2 obscured glass to selected patterns: D2, D6, D8.
The glass will be back and face puttied in approved mastic and secured with beads, sockets and screws as specified before.

15.06   Hack out any cracked, scratched or broken panes and replace, and on completion clean and polish all glass both sides.

Painting materials should always be specified against a reputable maker's paint system.

Primers vary for each substrate, and each one required should be described in full. Primer/sealer/undercoats should be avoided.

Knotting should be specified to the BS. Stopping should be as described. The use of putty is to be discouraged.

The general provisions of BS 6150: 1982 for workmanship should be enlarged to suit any particular or special requirements.

Two coats of knotting are advisable and all holes and defects should be filled after priming.

16.00 PAINTING AND DECORATING

16.01 Materials. The whole of the paints, unless otherwise specified, are to be manufactured by . . . and used strictly in accordance with the manufacturer's recommendations.

16.02 Primers. Primers to differing materials will be as follows:

Priming to softwood	lead-based primer to BS 2523: 1966
Priming to metalwork	zinc rich to BS 4652: 1971
Priming to bedding surfaces of natural finish timbers	aluminium primer to BS 4756: 1971
Priming to galvanized surfaces	calcium plumbate primer to BS 3698: 1964

16.03 Knotting is to be best quality, composed of shellac dissolved in methylated spirits only to BS 1336: 1971.

16.04 Stopping is to consist of white lead and gold size putty gauged to 1:3.

16.05 Workmanship. Workmanship generally is to comply with BS 6150: 1982. No external painting is to be carried out in wet or foggy weather or upon surfaces which are not thoroughly dry, and no painting on interior work will be permitted until the building has been rendered free from dust.

16.06 Two thin coats of knotting well brushed out are applied to all knotty, sappy or resinous areas to be painted.

16.07 All nail holes, cracks and defects are to be filled and levelled up with stopping.

16.08 All loose scale and rust is to be completely removed from iron and steel before painting and surface treated with Jenolite before priming.

16.09 All plasterwork is to be allowed to dry thoroughly and all traces of efflorescence removed before decorating is commenced.

16.10 All paints are to be used and mixed strictly to the manufacturer's instructions and are to be delivered in sealed containers. All tints are to be selected by the architect and the contractor is to allow for or include in his tender for supplying sample tints for approval and for finishing in parti-colours where directed.

16.11 Generally the contractor is to finally touch up and make good the decorations after all trades on completion, scrub all floors and pavings, clean and polish all unpainted metalwork, remove all paint splashes and leave the building clean and ready for occupation to the reasonable satisfaction of the architect.

The number of coats of paint to be applied to a surface will depend on the quality of the work and the amount of money available. Generally, on new work three coats is the minimum. Four coats will give more depth of finish and a longer life.

Natural finishes should be prepared, filled and applied precisely according to the maker's recommendations.

The specification clauses for drainage works will follow both maker's recommendations and Codes of Practice, varying with the basic materials used.

Flexibly jointed clayware drain pipes do not need a concrete bed and flaunching and can be laid satisfactorily on a granular bedding.
uPVC pipes jointed with ring seals and pitch-fibre pipes jointed in socketed polypropylene couplings are generally bedded in 19 mm quarry scappling, ballast or shingle.

Brick manholes are suitable for all pipe systems. uPVC can incorporate special manholes made in the same material and bedded and connected to the pipe runs as individual makers recommend.

16.12 Woodwork. All external woodwork to be painted is to be twice knotted, primed, stopped and painted with two undercoats and one coat gloss finish.

16.13 Natural Columbian pine is to be carefully rubbed down, filled to match, prepared and sealed with one coat matt Ronuk seal to manufacturer's instructions and twice wax-polished with clear natural wax.

16.14 The Oak door and frame shall be rubbed down to clean finish, scraped if so required, prepared and twice limed with addition of 5 per cent lamp black to approved colour.

16.15 Metalwork. Clean down, prime with correct primer as specified before, and paint with two undercoats and one coat gloss finish.

17.00 DRAINAGE

17.01 Materials. Clay pipes and fittings for drainage shall be to BS 65: 1981. Plain-ended British Standard quality should be used in foul sewage drains; Type 2 spigot and socketed British Standard surface water quality should be used for surface and storm water only.

17.02 Aggregates, sand, cement and concrete mixes shall be as specified before in concrete work.

17.03 Foul drain pipes shall be jointed with flexible mechanical joints to BS 6087: 1981 supplied by the pipe manufacturers and used strictly in accordance with their recommendations.

17.04 Surface water drains shall be jointed in gaskin and cement and sand (1:3) with a bold neat collar.

17.05 Workmanship. All drains shall be laid in straight runs to even and regular falls all as CP 301: 1971. Pipes under buildings and roadways and passing through walls shall be cased in 150 mm concrete Mix A. All stoneware pipes to foul drains shall be laid directly on the trimmed, natural trench bottom and, after testing, backfilled with 38 mm granular bedding material to crown of pipe and thence 2 no. 150 mm layers compacted by treading, the remainder of the fill placed and mechanically compacted. Surface water spigot and socketed pipes shall be laid on 100 mm concrete Mix A, flaunched up in concrete after testing and backfilled in selected excavated material.

17.06 Manholes. Form new manholes in positions shown on drawings with 100 mm concrete Mix A bottoms, 225 mm walls in Class B bricks to BS 3921: 1974 in cement mortar (1:3) internally neatly pointed and finished fair face, 100 mm concrete Mix B cover reinforced with 4 no. 9 mm m.s. bars each, perforated and rebated for and including 457 × 457 Ref.

Sewer connections are carried out by the local authority or water board responsible for the provision and maintenance of the sewer. To cover for the cost of cutting away for and providing and fixing the saddle connection carried out by their staffs a Provisional Sum is incorporated. The remainder of the work — opening up the sewer and providing the drain connection — is carried out by the contractor and must be specified to suit local conditions.

Gully specifications will vary to suit particular circumstances. Generally wastes should be discharged into a vertical back inlet to ensure they go into the gully under the grating.

Small domestic soakaways can be constructed as described. Large ones have a 150 mm concrete ring base, one-brick honeycomb walls in Class B bricks and concrete covers with access covers and frames.

The drainage should be tested twice lest damage during the progress of the contract be undiscovered on completion.

C6 – 18/18 Grade C (light duty) single-seal flat type inspection cover and frame to BS 497: 1976, the frames bedded and pointed up in cement mortar (1:3) and the covers set in manhole grease.

17.07   Provide and bed 100 mm clay half-round channels with all necessary three-quarters section branches and bench up in fine concrete rising 75 mm vertically from the channel and thence at an angle of 45 degrees. Render the benching in cement and sand (1:1) finished with a perfectly smooth face.

17.08   Connections. Include the Provisional Sum of £ _____ for connection to the local authority sewer in the road where indicated on the drawing.

17.09   Give notice to the local authority, take up pavement slabs and set aside for re-use, break up roadway, excavate for and expose sewer. Provide all necessary protection and lighting and backfill and reinstate carriageway, grass verge and pavement to the requirements and complete satisfaction of the local authority.
(Alternative clause providing connection to an existing manhole already connected to the local authority sewer or a common drain.)
Break through wall and benching of existing manhole as required, insert and bed new branch channel and make good to benching and wall of manhole.

17.10   Gullies. Provide and bed in position where shown on the drawings on 100 mm concrete Mix A base, 3 no. 150 x 150 clay two-piece gullies with square hopper top complete with black cast iron grating and vertical back inlet. Set gully tops 100 mm below top level of pavings, form sides in fine concrete with 25 mm thick cement and sand (1:1) skirting next wall, and joint gullies to drain.

17.11   Soakaways. Excavate for soakaways to sizes and depths below inlet shown on the drawings, fill in to 450 mm below finished ground level with approved broken brick hardcore, lay sheet of 1000 g polythene over and fill in over with topsoil up to finished ground level.

17.12   Generally. Make connections to all vent pipes, soil and vent pipes, WC outgoes and rainwater pipes with flexible joints and carry out all cutting and fitting required.

17.13   Provide all necessary plugs and equipment and test all drains to the requirements of the local authority and on completion of the contract in the presence of the architect to his complete satisfaction.

A general clause to cover materials and workmanship.

Pavement crossings are generally carried out either by the local highway authority or to their particular requirements; thus a Provisional Sum is appropriate.

While entrance steps and paving are required to a high standard, paths and terraces can be laid to a lower specification and should be described accordingly.

Drives can be as specified here or finished with 50 mm tarmacadam on to 100/150 mm hardcore base. The edging is common to both.

Gates can be specified out as shown or can form part of the Prime Cost Sum for fencing. Brick piers can be provided to carry wrot iron gates specified in Metalwork.

A general clause to clear and turn over the site and to bring up bats and other rubbish buried during the progress of the works.

18.00   EXTERNAL WORKS

18.01   <u>Generally</u>. Materials and workmanship are to comply with the previous trades where applicable and relevant to the work specified hereafter.

18.02   <u>Pavement crossover</u>. Include the Provisional Sum of £ _____ for pavement crossing complete.

18.03   <u>Front and rear entrance steps</u>. Excavate for as required, provide and lay 100 mm thick hardcore finished with 100 mm thick concrete Mix A set to fall away from the building and as shown on the drawings. Provide, bed and point up in cement and sand (1:3) 600 x 600 x 50 approved precast concrete paving slabs with neatly recessed joints.

18.04   <u>Paths and terrace</u>. Form paths and terrace where shown on the drawings, all as specified above but omitting concrete slab – precast slabs to be bedded on mortar dabs to consolidated hardcore base as described before.

18.05   <u>Drive</u>. Excavate 150 mm deep for new drive as shown on drawings and form edging of approved 50 x 150 square top precast concrete edging to BS 340: 1979 on 300 x 100 concrete Mix A bed, including flaunching up and pointing in cement and sand (1:3). Form base to drive of 150 mm thick approved consolidated brick hardcore and finish with 100 mm Chichester pea gravel properly levelled, rolled and consolidated to a level surface.

18.06   <u>Gate</u>. Provide, excavate for and set in 150 mm concrete Mix A all round, 175 x 175 <u>Oak</u> posts each 2.4 m long, bottom ends tarred and tops neatly weathered. Provide and hang to set of galvanized wrot iron double-strap top and bottom field gate hinges nutted and with square washers 1 no. <u>Oak</u> field gate 2.743 m wide to BS 3470: 1975 complete with galvanized wrot iron field gate catch comprising 610 mm spring head, 254 mm keep and catch.

18.07   <u>Fencing</u>. Include the Prime Cost Sum of £ _____ for close-boarded oak fencing, the work to be carried out by a specialist fencing contractor to be nominated by the architect. Add for profit and attendance.

18.08   <u>Turn over site</u>. Turn over site one spit deep from front boundary to back line of house and garage, generally level and clear and cart away from site all surplus soil and rubbish.

Ivor Brown, RIBA
Chartered Architect

8 September 1977

Schedule of	10.33	Prime Cost Sum of £ . . . for supply of kitchen fittings
Prime Cost	10.39	Prime Cost Sum of £ . . . for supply of ironmongery
and	12.17	Prime Cost Sum of £ . . . for heating installation
Provisional	12.19	Prime Cost Sum of £ . . . for supply of sanitary fittings
Sums	13.01	Prime Cost Sum of £ . . . for electrical installation
	14.07	Prime Cost Sum of £ . . . for wall tiling
	14.10	Prime Cost Sum of £ . . . for vinyl tiling
	14.11	Prime Cost Sum of £ . . . for wood block flooring
	2.00	Provisional Sum of £ . . . for contingencies
	6.13	Provisional Sum of £ . . . for fireplace
	10.32	Provisional Sum of £ . . . for wardrobe
	12.06	Provisional Sum of £ . . . for water and gas service connections
	12.16	Provisional Sum of £ . . . for drying out building
	12.18	Provisional Sum of £ . . . for builder's work
	17.07	Provisional Sum of £ . . . for sewer connection
	18.02	Provisional Sum of £ . . . for pavement crossover

9 Specifications for the use of the quantity surveyor

As we saw in Chapter 1, a specification may be required to amplify the information given in the drawings and to enable the quantity surveyor to measure the labour and materials more precisely to the architect's intentions. The specification does not form part of the contract but, after signature of the contract, it becomes an architect's instruction.

The use of this type of specification is therefore explanatory, and amplifies both drawings and quantities; it should be capable of giving the contractor information both as to the location of items and to their description. Many quantity surveyors, in lieu of a specification, tend to annotate their bills to provide this information – a common sign of slack and inefficient information provision by the architect.

The specification should follow the format laid down under SMM6 for the sequence and description of different trades (see page 53). This will enable cross-referencing from bill and specification of individual items and clauses, and will materially assist the builder in locating individual items in both documents. The descriptions should not be duplicated: the bill is both the tendering and the contractual document. However, quantities, aggregate materials and the specification should enable the builder to break quantities down into individual items and to distribute these to their respective positions. In addition, the precise quality and workmanship will be incorporated in expanded form in the preambles to the bill and need not be repeated in detail in the specification. Some specifications, before being typed or printed, are fully referenced to the bills by the insertion of the item number against each separate component in a similar manner to the annotation of a bill. This method, while time-consuming for the quantity surveyor, is better than annotation and is more popular with builders. Duplication of information already incorporated on the drawings should be avoided.

The information required by a quantity surveyor to prepare his bill can be set out as in the following example:

Glazing   Materials: Glass to BS 952, Pt 1: 1978
                             Putty to BS 544: 1969
           Workmanship: BS 6262: 1982
           Sheet glass: 4 mm
           Translucent glass: no. 1 fluted

To this can be added references to particular items in the bills after their preparation, as follows:

Glazing   Materials: Glass to BS 952, Pt 1: 1978 387—8
                      Putty to BS 544: 1969   389
        Workmanship: BS 6262: 1982   380—1
        Sheet glass: 4 mm   382
        Translucent glass: no. 1 fluted   383

This can be passed for typing and issued to site.

SMM6 not only provides the precise headings but also for specific information to be incorporated under each where appropriate. A draft specification for the quantity surveyor to be later issued for site use should be prepared on this basis, incorporating the following information. Reference should be made as required to Chapter 6 (BSS and CP applicable to building works).

General conditions and preliminaries
Contract form to be used
Preliminary particulars: project/parties
General facilities and attendance
Contingencies

SMM6 requirements in addition
Works by nominated subcontractors (Prime Cost Sums)
Attendance
Builder's work in connection
Goods and materials from nominated suppliers (Prime Cost Sums)
Works by public bodies (Provisional Sums)
Works by others directly engaged by the employer

These items can be incorporated in the different trade sections where required and collated by a schedule at the end of the specification.

Demolition
General items
Protection
Shoring, including needle prop and strut and other temporary works
Any special provision required for specialist works of repair or conservation

Excavation and earthwork
Generally:
Soil description if not indicated on the drawings
Site preparation — removing trees/hedges/lifting turf
Excavation
Earthwork supports where required

Disposal of water
Disposal of excavated material
Filling — hardcore/chalk/hogging/weak concrete
Surface treatment/truing and compaction
Protection of excavations and isolated holes

Notes   Filling to excavations from demolitions should be well-compacted hardcore under buildings and pavings.
Extra excavations below levels shown on drawings should be filled in with concrete
(state mix) if required.
Hardcore can be broken or crushed stone/hogging/chalk or similar material depending
on local circumstances and supply.

Concrete work   Incoporates Piling and Diaphragm walling if required:

Piling
Diaphragm walls
Protection

Generally:

Plant/r.c. structures/steel frame protection
In situ concrete
Reinforcement
Formwork
Precast concrete
Composition construction
Hollow block suspended construction
Pre-stressed concrete work
Protection

Notes   The type of cement should refer to soil conditions, e.g. sulphate-resisting to BS 4027:
1980.
Special concrete mixes should be substituted if required.
Specialist reinforcement should be specified or Prime Cost Sum included for supply and
fixing.
Any special requirements for formwork/striking in sequence/retaining props should be
specified.
Reinforcement for concrete beds should be incorporated where required, e.g. fabric to
BS 4483: 1969, specifying cover (usually on to 50 mm blinding when cast as oversite).
Pre-stressed lintels should be specified as from a nominated supplier, or a PC Sum included.

Brickwork and blockwork
Classification of work/foundations/load-bearing/non-load-bearing/facing brickwork/kind and size/bond/mortar/labours and specials/mortars
Brick facework — kind/size/mortars and pointing
Brickwork to boiler bases and chimney shafts
Blockwork
Damp courses
Sundries
Protection

Notes
Blocks will be specified to suit situation and thermal requirements and mortars to suit.
Wall ties specified to suit requirements, e.g. butterfly/vertical twists/double triangle to BS 1243: 1978.
Mortars will be specified as appropriate for the particular bricks used and their situation and pointing ditto.
Damp-proof courses specified to particular type required to BS 743: 1970.
Special bricks or bonds shall be specified separately.

Underpinning, shown as a separate trade in SMM6, can be incorporated as a 'work in all trades' item in this section.

Rubble walling and masonry
Rubble walling
   Stone/mortar/jointing
   Sundries/grooves/chases/holes/building in
   Centering
   Protection
Masonry
   Natural stonework/mortar/jointing
   Cast stone work
   Terracotta work
   Sundries (see above)
   Centering
   Protection

Notes
Stone for solid walling is drafted at back for economy.
Quarry or merchant should be specified, as well as particulars of bed, colour, finish.
Classification of stone, e.g. rubble/block in course/ashlar, should be specified.
Mortar should be specified to suit particular stone and situation.
Ashlar should be covered with stone grout as protection, this cleaned off on completion.

Rubble and masonry are separated in SMM6 but can be combined in the specification for ease of description.

Asphalt work   Mastic asphalt/sheathing felt as required/number of layers/finish
Sundries/fillets/drips/working into luting flanges/dressing over aprons and to lead/under
cutting
Asbestos tiling
Protection

Notes   Three layers always used — 28 mm thick to roofs and slopes not exceeding 30 degrees;
20 mm thick to vertical and slopes exceeding 30 degrees.
Angle fillets in two coats 50 mm wide to all internal angles.
Horizontal joints to be staggered 150 mm and in vertical work, 75 mm.
Free edges of asphalt always dressed into chase in vertical wall.
Asphalt for tanking should always be applied over roughened or bitumen-primed surface.
Vertical surfaces of asphalt can be applied over expanded metal lath to provide key.
Pipes passing through asphalt should have a tight non-ferrous sleeve and a mastic collar
run up the pipe with weathered top and angle fillet at foot.

Roofing
(including
vertical
cladding)   Slate or tile roofing/kind/size/side or end laps/fixing/laths and battens/pitch/labours/
eaves/verge/valleys/ridge/hips and special fittings/hip irons/slates, soakers and saddles
to *fix only*/underlay
Corrugated and trough sheet roofing and cladding
Roof decking
Bitumen felt roofing
Sheet metal roofing
Sheet metal flashings and gutters/material/gauge/quality
Protection

Notes   Tiles or slates must be particularized and supplier or maker named.
Battens and laths must be treated with a preservative/size of battens will depend on tile
used and span between rafters.
Fittings to be provided will relate to tile or slate used and must conform to manufacturers
instructions or specific tradition (tiles).
Corrugated or troughed roofing and roof decking must be provided with supporting
purlins at centres recommended by the manufacturer. Use approved fixings/access-
ories and fittings.
Sheet metal roofing must be laid on a solid deck with a separating layer of felt to BS 747:
1977. The specification must follow the appropriate Code of Practice for the
particular metal employed.

Woodwork   Material/finish/treatment/selection/matching/surface treatment during manufacture/sizing
Carcassing
First fixings/boards and flooring/second fixings/skirtings and architraves

Composite items/trussed rafters/doors/door frames and lining sets/casement doors and windows/staircases/balustrades

Sundries/plugging/holes/insulation/metalwork

Ironmongery

Protection

Notes   Quality and sizes of timber for joinery and grade for structural use must be specified.

Preservative treatment should be described.

Species of timber for structural work and hardwood for joinery should be described.

Workmanship should either be to BS for joinery or precisely described.

Carcassing work should have joints precisely specified together with fixings, bolts, straps, etc.

Standard stock items of joinery should be specified to the type number and appropriate BS.

Treatment of bedding faces and priming of joinery before delivery should be noted.

Items from specialist suppliers should be fully described together with details of supplier.

Ironmongery can be PC Sum or fully described against nominated supplier's list or catalogue. Always give finish and any special requirements.

Structural steelwork   General classification – unfabricated steel sections/fabricated steelwork

Steelwork/grades/method of fabrication/tests/designation by serial or size and weight

Fittings/connections and anchorages

Painting and surface treatment

Erection

Protection

Notes   Material should be specified to BS 4 or appropriate and fabrication to BS 449 and supplement.

Important to fully describe protection against corrosion especially if steel is exposed to be painted.

Preparation to be to BS 5493: 1977.

Metalwork   Kind of metal/gauge/off-site protection

Composite items/fabricated off-site/windows and doors/rooflights/laylights/pavement lights/balustrades and staircases/duct covers/gates/grilles

Plates/floor plates/frames/bearers/mat well frames

Sheet metal/wire mesh/expanded metal

Bolts/screws/rivets

Protection

Notes See structural steelwork for materials, fabrication and protection where applicable.

Galvanized materials should, where a painted finish is applied, be primed with a plumbate primer for preference.

Galvanizing or zinc spraying should be carried out after manufacture to BS 2569, Pt 1: 1964.

Specify method of assembly or fixing, e.g. welding/bolting/riveting, and specify countersunk, cup or hexagonal.

Plumbing and mechanical engineering installations

Gutterwork/pipework and rainwater pipes
Ductwork
Equipment/chimneys/elements/supports
Insulation
Sundries
Builder's work
Protection

Notes Most work in this section is covered by Prime Cost and Provisional Sums.

Gutterwork should describe material, profile, jointing and fixing required and details of manufacturer or appropriate BS.

Any special requirements for drying out the building can be included here.

Electrical installations

Regulations/materials/testing/voltage
Fixing/temporary work/description of installation/location
Equipment and control gear
Fittings and accessories
Conduit/trunking/cable trays
Cables
Circuits/sub-circuits
Earthing
Ancillaries/identification plates
Sundries/disconnection and re-connection and refixing of equipment/testing/circuit diagrams
Builder's work
Protection

Notes The work is generally covered by Prime Cost and Provisional Sums. Builder's work can be a problem; for example, many electrical firms carry out their own chasing while relying on the contractor to provide certain backboards, holes for trunking and cable tray supports, etc. This should be clarified with the subcontractors.

Floor, wall and ceiling finishes

General description of work

In situ finishes/materials/walls ceilings, beams and columns/mouldings staircase areas/ floors/channels/skirtings and kerbs/dividing strips/labours

Beds and backing

Tile, slab and block finishings

Mosaic work

Flexible sheet finishings — general description/wall and ceiling finishes/floor finishes/labours

Dry linings and partitions

Suspended ceilings, linings and support work

Fibrous plaster — wall and ceiling coverings/arches and domes/casings to beams/covers and cornices/consoles and canopies/models

Fitted carpeting and underlay

Protection

Notes

Much of the work is of a specialist nature and would be the subject of Prime Cost Sums.

In situ finishes would include granolithic and asphaltic finishes.

Plastering to walls, etc. should specify standard of workmanship and detail precise requirements of materials to appropriate BSS.

Where required details of expanded metal beads and quirks should be given together with precise locations.

Floor finishes are generally the subject of Prime Cost Sums. Their locations and distribution should be indicated on Schedules of Finishes. Care should be taken to describe parting strips and protection.

Glazing

Classification of work/grouped with kind and quality of glass

Glass in openings

Leaded lights

Mirrors

Patent glazing

Dome lights

Protection

Notes

Workmanship should be specified to BS 6262: 1982.

Glass should be specifically described together with appropriate bedding compound to suit frame material. Reference to a glazing or window schedule is advisable.

Mirrors should be protected by use of distance pieces at the back to keep glass off wall surface.

All glass should be cleaned on completion and scratched, cracked or broken panes replaced.

Painting and decorating

Description of work classified into: new work internally; new work externally
Repainting and redecoration internally
Repainting and redecoration externally
Work before finishing specifically described: painting/polishing/graining
Sign writing
Decorative paper
Protection

Notes

Workmanship to be to BS 6150: 1982 generally and to the selected manufacturer's recommendations.
Either specify materials to the appropriate BS or explicitly select their manufacturers.
Any repainting work should have old paint either burnt off, if it is flaking or defective, or well rubbed down and prepared if its condition is suitable for re-coating.
Decorative papers are usually the subjects of PC Sums.

Drainage

Nature of ground
Pipe trenches/excavation/disposal of water/beds, backing and coverings/pipework
Manholes/soakaways/cesspits/septic tanks
Connections to sewers
Testing drains
Protection

Notes

Workmanship to be to CP 301: 1971 and to the recommendations of the manufacturer of the pipe material selected.
Materials should be described to the appropriate BS relating also to the manufacturer.
Sewerage works and septic tanks, etc., generally incorporate a Prime Cost Sum for plant and equipment *plus* builder's work to manufacturer's drawings and requirements.
Connection to sewer is generally covered by a Provisional Sum.

Fencing and external works

Open-type fencing — post and wire/post and rail/chainlink and wire mesh/cleft pole/ pallisade/metal bar
Close-type fencing — close-boarded/built up concrete/corrugated
Gates
Sundries/concrete spurs/special posts/holes and mortises for posts
Protection

Notes

While SMM6 incorporates Site and External works in the various trades or sections of the bill it is often appropriate and advisable to separate the specification for the work.
Fencing and gates are usually specialist items covered by Prime Cost Sums. There may well be builder's work, e.g. gate piers, which need to be specified.

10 Specifications for alteration works

Specifications for alteration works are presented in a different form from those written for new works. The trade format which is regarded as suitable for the latter is of little help to either the estimator, the builder or the supervising architect. Consequently, while the general principles of contract are still applicable, the layout is changed to suit the different conditions which apply in contracts for alteration works.

The general principles for all specifications incorporate: the contract form; general preliminary clauses; material and workmanship clauses incorporating work clauses prepared in trade sections and sequence. In Chapter 8 we saw how these are presented for the new works. This form is also applicable for specifications prepared to amplify the bills of quantity. With specifications for alteration works the multitude of small items of a similar nature spread throughout the building, and the need to locate these precisely to specific rooms, has led to a format which extracts the whole of the general material and workmanship clauses from the main body of the specifications and groups these in trade format order in a separate section immediately following the preliminaries. As a result time is saved in preparing writing the specification, and the document itself is shorter. Specifications for alteration works are divided into:

The contract form
Preliminaries
Material and workmanship clauses set out in trade sequence
Work clauses

In addition the last section, Work clauses, may well be subdivided into a number of appropriate sections depending on the nature of the works. For example, it might well be appropriate to separate the clauses relating to pulling down and demolition if there are extensive works in this field that are likely to be sublet. External works and drainage might well be separated and a separate section devoted to Prime Cost, Provisional Sums and associated attendance and builder's work. However, each contract will be assessed individually and the specification written to suit its particular needs.

In Chapter 7 we saw how clauses are prepared and presented to cover the requirements of the contract form and general preliminary items relating to the works. This form is practical and also suitable for specifications for alteration works. The relevant clauses are selected to suit both the contract conditions and the work involved. For example:

1   Selection of contract form

JCT Standard Form of Building Contract (1980), Private, Without Qualities, *or*
JCT Agreement for Minor Building Works, January 1980

2 Preliminaries
Clause 2.01 (VAT requirements)
Clause 2.02 (improvement grant work, etc., only)
Clause 2.06 (trial holes — may be omitted)
Clause 2.09 Water (alternative to be selected)
etc.

The third section of the specification will incorporate such material and workmanship clauses as are required for the works, preferably set out in trade sequence. This format is readily accepted by the builder because the sequence is familiar; he will find it more acceptable than a loose and varied jumble of unconnected clauses. Follow the sequence used in specifications for new works (see Chapter 4). The example in this chapter for the general specification of works is given with a commentary on the suggested text.

The general specification example is followed by an example of work clauses for the conversion of a detached, two-storey Victorian house into two self-contained flats. This example shows the wide variety of type clauses relating to additions, alterations and repairs and indicates a method which may be used to specify works of this nature. As each contract is unique in its separate requirements, so each specification clause is, in itself, unique. There is no commentary to this section which, in the main, is self-explanatory.

This shows the use of a standard heading which provides all the information required for estimating and contracting purposes. The specification should be dated and the architect's name and address included.

Alternative clauses are given for general excavation. In most cases, general excavation over the whole site to a depth of 150 mm would be required but where the existing and finished levels are precisely indicated on the drawings the *alternative* clause would be appropriate. If hardcore is to be used the hardcore is described *otherwise* concrete blinding.

A general clause covering excavation for foundation trenches incorporating preparation of the bottom to receive concrete and r.f.r. after the foundation concrete and walls have been constructed.
A similar clause to that for foundation trenches but incorporates extra labours to fall and gradients specifically required in drainage trenches.

Another general clause to deal with excavations required for trenches for services specified later in the document.

A general clause to keep excavations free from water.

A general clause to ensure removal of surplus soil from the site. The *alternative* clause deals with the retention of valuable topsoil and its disposition on site.

Specification of works to be carried out and materials to be used in alterations and additions to form two self-contained flats at No. 27, Horndean Road, London SE4 for J. Dimes, Esq., to the reasonable satisfaction of the architect.

November 1976

Ivor Brown, RIBA
Chartered Architect
13 Lewes Road, Luton

1.00 GENERAL CONDITIONS
(See Chapter 7 for alternative clauses for insertion dealing with the appropriate contract form.)

2.00 PRELIMINARIES
(See Chapter 7 for alternative clauses for insertion dealing with preliminary items.)

3.00 GENERAL SPECIFICATION OF WORKS

3.01 <u>Excavation and earthwork.</u> Excavate over the whole area of the works and pavings to an average depth of 150 mm, level and consolidate bottoms to receive hardcore.
    Or, use this alternative clause:
Excavate over the whole area of the works and pavings to reduced levels shown on the drawings, level and consolidate bottoms to receive hardcore (or weak concrete blinding, etc.).

3.02 Excavate trenches for foundations to the widths and depths shown on the drawings, level and consolidate bottoms for concrete, return, fill in and consolidate well selected excavated material around footings.

3.03 Excavate for drain runs, manholes and gullies as shown on the drawings to required levels and falls, grade and consolidate bottoms, and return, fill in and consolidate on completion. Break in tops of trenches under floors and pavings to three times their width.

3.04 Excavate for services and service connections as shown on the drawings or specified hereafter and return, fill in and consolidate on completion.

3.05 Keep all excavations free from water at all times by pumping or baling as required.

3.06 Wheel and cart away to tip all surplus excavated material unless specified hereafter to the contrary.
    Or, use this alternative clause:

General description of permitted material to make up levels under oversite concrete and external pavings where required and specified. Alternatives are given for the d.p.m. over the hardcore filling and must be deleted depending on the architect's direction.

The general clause for cement giving *alternative* for sulphate-resisting quality.

A general clause for fine aggregate and sand for concreting.

A general clause for coarse aggregate and ballast for concreting.

A general clause covering a number of common concrete mixes in use. This may need to be varied subject to the structural engineer's requirements.

A general clause dealing with the method of mixing concrete and controlling the quality of water and the consistency.

This clause ensures that the concrete is placed and consolidated while still in good condition.

A general clause dealing with the construction of formwork and requirements for striking. Also alternative methods open to the contractor for ensuring a fair face where required.

A general clause dealing with the quality, fixing and cover required for bar and mesh reinforcement in r.c. work.

Wheel and deposit all topsoil in heap where indicated on drawings for re-use in garden works, and wheel and cart away to tip all surplus excavated material.

3.07   Hardcore will be approved clean brick, stone, concrete or hoggin, broken as required to pass a 75 mm ring, made up to reduced levels in layers not exceeding 150 mm, well consolidated, levelled, blinded with fine material and finished with a layer of building paper to BS 1521: 1972 Type B2 (or 500 g polythene sheet) as shown on the drawings, edges lapped minimum of 150 mm and turned up full thickness of concrete around the perimeter of the slab.

3.08   Concrete work. Cement for concreting will generally be normal setting quality to BS 12: 1978. Where specified, hereafter, to be sulphate-resisting, cement will conform to BS 4027: 1980.

3.09   Fine aggregate shall consist of well-graded, clean, sharp pit or river sand complying with BS 882, Pt 2: 1973, not more than 5 per cent failing to pass a 4.76 mm sieve.

3.10   Coarse aggregate will consist of natural gravel, crushed gravel or stone complying with BS 882, Pt 2: 1973, and of the nominal sizes stated.

3.11   Concrete mixes will be as follows:

Mix A – one part cement to seven parts all in aggregate to pass 38 mm sieve
Mix B – one part cement to two parts fine aggregate to four parts coarse aggregate to pass 19 mm sieve
Mix C – one part cement to seven parts all in aggregate to pass a 19 mm sieve
Mix D – one part cement to twelve parts all in aggregate to pass 38 mm sieve

3.12   Concrete may be mixed by hand on a clean, boarded platform, mixed by machine or delivered to site ready-mixed with only sufficient water added to give a good workable mix of uniform colour, consistency and a slump not exceeding 50 mm.

3.13   All concrete will be placed in position and properly consolidated as rapidly as possible after mixing; no throwing or dropping will be allowed.

3.14   Formwork is to be solidly and rigidly constructed to carry the weight of wet concrete without deflection. Concrete specified fair face will be cast against hardboard or plywood-lined formwork. No formwork will be struck until agreed by the architect.

3.15   Hot rolled steel bar reinforcement will comply with BS 4449: 1978 and steel fabric to BS 4483: 1969 and supplied free from oil, dirt or loose rust. All to be properly fixed in position to a minimum cover of 25 mm on slabs, 38 mm on columns and 50 mm on foundations, all intersections of bars secured with soft galvanized wire, all fabric lapped 150 mm and wired and all bars to have hooked ends or lapped minimum 30D.

A general clause covering all necessary labours to concrete in respect of other trades.

A general clause giving alternative methods by which the specification of bricks can be affected.

Facing bricks are best described in this way rather than by alternative use of a PC Sum as described in Chapter 4.

Lightweight or insulating blocks for partitions are best specified by thickness, the relevant BS and the manufacturer.

Wall ties should be to the relevant BS as shown, and the type selected should be given.

A general clause describing mortar mixes and their use and application in the works.

The precise requirements as to pointing must be specified: tuck, struck, ironed, etc., as required.

The precise material and fixing of the damp-proof course is essential not only to the base of the wall but also to reveals. The latter can be varied to slate in cement mortar or using Davatic cavity closing.

A general clause covering the construction of the walls and the bond to be employed.

A requirement of the Building Regulations in external cavity walling.

A general clause dealing with the various labours additional to the above to cover cavity walling and its protection from damp penetration.

3.16   Form all holes, sinkings and mortises as required in the concrete by other trades as the work proceeds or cut away for and make good after.

3.17   Brickwork and blockwork. Common bricks will be clay to BS 3921: 1974 Class B for use below damp-proof course and in manholes and Class 1 above.
or
Common bricks will be calcium silicate to BS 187: 1978 Class 3 for use below damp-proof course and Class 1 above.

3.18   Facing bricks will be . . . manufactured by . . ., generally to BS 3921: 1974 and approved in bulk by the architect before delivery.

3.19   Partitions where shown on drawings (coloured green) and inner leaves of cavity walls will be 100 mm (or state thickness) precast concrete blocks to BS 6073, Pt 1: 1981, manufactured by . . . .

3.20   Wall ties will be galvanized butterfly (double triangle/vertical twist) type to BS 1243: 1978 set every 900 mm horizontally and 450 mm vertically with extra at reveals, corners and below wall plate.

3.21   Mortar below d.p.c. and above roof level will be cement and sand 1:3. Mortar for lightweight block partitions will be cement, lime and sand 1:1:9. Otherwise mortar will be 1:1:6. Mortar will be fresh for each day's work and knocking up will not be permitted.

3.22   Pointing will be carried out as the work proceeds with the joint cut off flush with the trowel and lightly brushed.

3.23   Damp-proof courses will be bitumen-based Type A (state type otherwise) to BS 743: 1970, the full width of the wall and lapped a minimum of 100 mm. All cavities will be closed at reveals with a 225 mm strip tacked to the back of the timber frame (100 mm strip dressed into metal frame) and set to pass into the cavity. All timber sills to be bedded on 100 mm strip of d.p.c.
or
Damp-proof course will be Hyload Pitch Polymer manufactured by Ruberoid Building Products Ltd and used strictly in accordance with the manufacturer's recommendations.

3.24   The walls are to be built to the heights, thicknesses and dimensions shown on the drawings, rising four courses to 300 mm, perpends properly kept, arrises true and courses true and level. The bond will be stretcher (English, Flemish, etc.) or as specified hereafter.

3.25   Provide and fill cavity with fine concrete filling up to ground level with splayed top and weepholes every fourth perpend.

3.26   Build in wall ties as the work proceeds, leave sand courses over trays, keep cavities free from mortar droppings, clear all ties and trays of mortar and build up sand courses

A general clause covering all the general labours involved in ancillary works relating to brick and blockwork.

A general clause dealing with the bonding of blockwork to block and brickwork, the building in of items to partitions, and, in addition, general attendance on other trades requiring mortising and cutting.

Roofing generally is specified in the work clauses and this general item is merely a general clause regarding proper and perfect completion.

A general clause dealing with the preservative treatment of timber, its strength and measurement characteristics, both for carcassing and joinery.

A general clause ensuring the best possible workmanship for carpentry subject to the skill of the workman.

A general clause dealing with the proper procedure of work, protection and fixing of joinery.

A general clause covering the priming of trim and joinery before fixing.

A general clause ensuring that steelwork complies with the 'deemed to satisfy' requirements of the Building Regulations and that it will be properly prepared and primed after manufacture.

A general clause specifying the preparation and treatment of general metalwork before installation in the building, as well as the special priming required for galvanized items requiring painting.

A clause specifying quality and general workmanship for plumbers leadwork.

on completion.

3.27 Build in concrete and all other lintels specified, build in all horizontal and vertical d.p.c.s, lead trays, flashings and chimney safes, and point up as required on completion, using mastic around all window and door frames and leave weepholes where required every fourth perpend.

3.28 Blockbond all partitions to new and existing walls, build in all frames and frame ties, joist hangers, matwell frames, carry out all cutting and fitting required, attend upon, cut away for and make good after all trades.

3.29 Roofing. Clean out all gutters, remove all bitumen marks, replace any cracked or damaged tiles (slates) and leave all roofs perfect and watertight on completion.

3.30 Woodwork. Timber for carcassing will be treated in accordance with BS 4072: 1966, will comply in all respects with CP 112, Pt 2: 1971 measurement of characteristics being measured in accordance with BS 4978: 1973.
Timber for joinery will be 'unsorted' grade treated in accordance with BS 4072: 1974, and be selected in accordance with BS 1186, Pt 2: 1971.
Sawn timber will hold to the sizes specified, 2 mm being allowed for each sawn face. Reduction of basic size by preparation shall be in accordance with BS 4471, Pt 1: 1978.

3.31 All structural timbers are to be framed together in the best possible manner and to include all nails, bolts, hangers, connectors and straps required.

3.32 Door and window frames are to be built in as the work proceeds, knotted and primed on all faces before fixing and well protected. All horns trimmed on site are to have bare wood re-primed. Sheradized pressed-steel fixing cramps are to be screwed to the backs of all frames and built in every eight courses of brickwork.

3.33 All fascias, weatherboarding, skirtings, linings and architraves are to be knotted and primed on all faces before fixing.

3.34 Structural steelwork. All structural steelwork will be from steel to BS 4, Pt 1: 1980 and fabricated in accordance with BS 449, Pt 2: 1969. All steel will be free from all loose rust and scale and primed with two coats of primer before hoisting and fixing.

3.35 Metalwork. All iron and steel items, unless galvanized during manufacture, are to be prepared and primed with two coats before installation. Exposed galvanized items are to be treated with a mordant solution and primed with calcium plumbate before fixing.

3.36 Plumbing and mechanical engineering services. Sheet lead is to be best milled to BS 1178: 1982. The material is to be of the thickness specified, well and neatly dressed without injury to the surface, with provision made for expansion and contraction without injury. All nails used will be copper.

A clause specifying the standard of copper pipework both as regards acceptable material and fittings and the applicable regulations.

A general clause specifying the requirements of pipe lagging in voids and roof spaces.

A general clause covering uPVC gutters and r.w.p.s which can be amended to suit the appropriate material to be used in the works.

The various materials approved for this work can be selected and specified against the appropriate BS.

A general clause inserted when the electrical specification is specified rather than covered by the inclusion of a Prime Cost Sum.

A general clause to cover the protection of internal finishes and their cleanliness on completion of the works.

A number of general clauses dealing with the specific requirements, storage, workmanship and protection of plastered surfaces to walls and ceilings.

A general clause covering the bedding and pointing of glazed wall tiles.

A general clause dealing with general workmanship, protection, curing and replacement of defective floor screeds.

A number of general clauses dealing with the quality of glass and bedding compounds, the preparation, standards of workmanship, cleaning and replacement of broken or defective glass.

3.37   All pipework will be copper to BS 2871, Pt 2: 1972 with approved compression (capillary) fittings and carried out in accordance with the Building Regulations and the requirements of the local water authority.

3.38   All pipes in roof spaces and voids will be lagged to CP 99: 1972 with Super Foamflex pipe insulation fixed in accordance with the manufacturer's instructions.

3.39   Gutters and rainwater pipes will be uPVC to BS 4576, Pt 1: 1970 manufactured by . . . and fixed in accordance with the manufacturer's recommendations.

3.40   The one pipe soil and vent shafts will be 100 mm diameter uPVC to BS 4514: 1983 (asbestos cement/pitch impregnated fibre/cast iron) installed, jointed and fixed strictly to BS 5572: 1978 and the manufacturer's recommendations.

3.41   The whole of the plumbing, heating and hot-water installation will be tested on completion to the approval of the architect.

3.42   Electrical installation. The electrical installation will be carried out in accordance with the latest IEE Regulations and tested on completion to the approval of the architect.

3.43   Floor, wall and ceiling finishes. Carefully protect all applied floor, wall and ceiling finishes, cover up all floors and pavings and leave clean and perfect on completion of the works.

3.44   All materials are to be as specified and stored in approved dry conditions on delivery to site.

3.45   Plasterboard lath is to be of the thickness specified, fixed to the manufacturer's recommendations, junctions with walls properly scrimmed.

3.46   All plastered walls and ceilings are to be finished straight, smooth and true, free from dents and other defects.

3.47   All external angles except window reveals to be provided with expanded metal beads.

3.48   All glazed tiles to be bedded in waterproof bedding compound and pointed up in white grout.

3.49   All floor screeds are to be well tamped, consolidated and bedded. Cover up, protect and properly cure and hack up and relay any hollow or defective areas.

3.50   Glazing. All sheet glass is to be OG quality of British manufacture to BS 952, Pt 1: 1978, free from scratches and all other imperfections.

3.51   Putty for wood casements is to be linseed oil to BS 544: 1969 and for metal windows to be approved metal glazing compound.

A number of general clauses dealing with the materials, methods of application and workmanship for painting and decoration to both internal and external surfaces.

The materials for drainage work will generally be shown on the drawings, but if not, they will need to be specified to the appropriate BS as described in the appropriate alternative clauses.

3.52   All rebates are to be primed before glazing, all glass cut to fit easily into the rebates, properly back puttied, sprigged or clipped and puttied the full depth of the rebate and sight lines and neatly cleaned off on completion.

3.53   All glass is to be left clean and polished both sides. Any cracked or broken panes to be hacked out and renewed and the whole of the glazing left clean and perfect on completion.

3.54   Painting and decorating. Primers, paints and emulsions generally will be manufactured by . . . and used strictly in accordance with their recommendations.

3.55   No external painting will be carried out in wet, foggy or frosty weather, or when the surfaces are not thoroughly dry, or internally before the premises are rendered free from dust.

3.56   All knots and resinous areas of timber are to be twice treated with shellac knotting to BS 1336 : 1971 before priming and all nail holes, cracks and defects properly filled and levelled up with hard stopping.

3.57   All loose scale and rust is to be completely removed from bare iron and steel surfaces before application of the specified primer.

3.58   All new plaster is to be throughly dry and free from efflorescence and the surface lightly rubbed down before painting.

3.59   Each coat of gloss or eggshell paint except the last is to be lightly rubbed down and the surface cleansed before the next coat is applied. All tints are to be as directed by the architect.

3.60   The patterns for all wallpapers will be selected by the architect. All papers shall be hung vertically and all pieces matched with neatly butted joints. No heading joints will be allowed and any lengths stained or damaged shall be replaced and the whole left perfect to the approval of the architect.

3.61   Touch up and make good all decorations after all trades on completion, clean and polish all unpainted metalwork, remove all paint splashes and leave the whole works clean and perfect to the approval of the architect.

3.62   Drainage. Foul and stormwater drains will be of the materials specified and shown on the drawings, laid and jointed in accordance with the manufacturer's recommendations. All pipes will be laid in straight runs and even and regular falls between manholes.

3.63   Drains will be formed from . . . diameter pitch-fibre pipes and fittings to BS 2760 : 1973, laid jointed and connected strictly to the manufacturer's recommendations.
        or
        Drains will be formed from . . . diameter plain end vitrified clay pipes and fittings

A series of general specification clauses dealing with the construction of traditional brick and concrete manholes, generally used in small work projects. The use of precast concrete or plastic manholes would require amended specification clauses to suit the manufacturer's recommendations.

Access covers to internal manholes are generally double-seal pattern to Table 7, Grade C, unless cast-iron bolted access covers are provided. Table 8, Grade C and Table 9 Grade C, are suitable for filling in with paving material to match surrounding, covers to Table 9 also being double-seal pattern.

Flexible connections are preferable to rigid to allow for movement and settlement.

A general clause covering the mandatory requirement of testing under the Building Regulations. Testing on completion is to ensure that any damage caused after filling in by vehicles on the site is located and rectified within the contract.

with polypropylene couplings to BS 65: 1981, laid, jointed and connected strictly to the manufacturer's recommendations.
or
Soil drains under buildings will be formed from . . . diameter cast iron spigot and socketed drain pipes and fittings to BS 437: 1978, laid, jointed and connected in accordance with CP 301: 1971.
or
Soil drains will be formed from . . . diameter uPVC underground drain pipes and fittings to BS 4660: 1973, laid and jointed in accordance with the manufacturer's recommendations and the relevant portions of CP 301: 1971.

3.64   All manholes to be constructed with 225 mm walls below 0.9 m of Class B bricks to BS 3921: 1974, bedded and pointed in cement mortar 1:3 to the depths and dimensions shown on 100 mm concrete Mix A base with 100 mm concrete Mix C cover reinforced with 4 no. 10 mm m.s. bars and rebated and perforated for cast iron cover.

3.65   Provide and bed in cement mortar 1:3 . . . mm diameter brownware half-round channels and three-quarters-section branches, bench up vertically 75 mm above edge of channel and thence at 45 degrees to manhole wall. Neatly point up brickwork internally fair face and render the benching in cement and sand 1:1 with a perfectly smooth face.

3.66   Access covers to manholes will be . . . mm x . . . mm cast iron light (medium) duty covers and frames to BS 497: 1976 Table 6 − Grade 6 painted two coats black bitumastic paint before fixing, frame bedded in cement and sand 1:3 and the cover in approved manhole grease.

3.67   Gullies are to be as specified hereafter set on 100 mm concrete Mix A base and cased after testing. Form curb to gullies of brick on edge in cement mortar 1:3 (approved precast concrete) with 25 mm rendered skirting against external wall of building.

3.68   Make all connections to vent pipes, S & VPs, gullies, WC pans, etc., with flexible connections, and carry out all cutting and fitting required.

3.69   Provide all necessary plugs and test the whole of the drainage when laid and again on completion to the requirements and satisfaction of the architect and the local authority. Any lengths, fittings or construction found to be faulty to be taken up, relaid or reconstructed and re-tested until satisfactory. Testing will be by water, generally as required by CP 301: 1971.

4.00   WORK TO FORM NEW BATHROOM EXTENSION

4.01   Demolition
  (i)   Carefully take down existing timber-framed temporary store complete, break up existing concrete floor, clear and cart away from site.

(ii) Carefully take down existing r.w.p. waste head and waste pipe and set aside on site for re-use.

(iii) Take down existing gutter and fascia complete to north elevation and clear away from site.

(iv) Remove existing door and frame, cut away concrete sill for future floor finish as required, clear and cart away from site.

(v) Remove existing cement fillet at verge, remove existing verge and eaves slates as necessary and prepare for making out for new slated roof.

(vi) Remove existing air brick and WC window complete, cut and prepare indents for bonding all new work to old, clear and cart away all rubbish.

4.02 <u>Foundations</u>. Excavate and form foundations of concrete Mix A levelled and prepared to receive brickwork. Fill cavity with concrete Mix C to within 150 mm of d.p.c. and weather top to weepholes.

4.03 <u>Brickwork</u>. Form walls as shown on drawings with approved Class B bricks in cement mortar up to d.p.c. level and thence with inner skin of Thermalite or equal and approved blocks in compo mortar (1:1:9) and facing skin of second London stocks in compo mortar (1:1:6) jointed and pointed to match existing work.

4.04 <u>Lintels</u>. Provide, hoist, bed and build into walls standard D/L lintels 150 mm deep with a minimum bearing of 150 mm at each end to windows W1 and W2 complete with splayed 150 x 150 concrete Mix B lintels each reinforced with 1 No. 13 mm m.s. bars and with layer of 12 mm polystyrene between metal and concrete.

4.05 <u>Windows</u>. Provide and fix in accordance with the manufacturer's instructions 2 no. Crittal M4 galvanized steel windows type 5 V4, glazed in narrow Reedlyte in metal glazing compound complete with brick sill set weathered and projecting 50 mm and rendered in compo mortar 19 mm thick. Render out sill internally and finish with white glazed bullnose tiles pointed in white cement.

4.06 <u>Ground floor</u>. Excavate to reduced levels, level and ram bottom, provide and lay brick hardcore broken to 75 mm ring, well consolidated and blinded with fine material. Provide and lay 100 mm concrete Mix B on layer of 1000 gauge polythene turned up at edges and prepare surface of concrete for and paint two coats Tretolastic bitumen waterproof membrane allowing twenty-four hours between each coat. Prepare and lay 38 mm cement and sand (1:3) screed well consolidated and tamped and levelled and lay 2 mm Armstrong Arlon vinyl tiles of pattern as directed by the architect, including all cutting and waste.

4.07 <u>First floor</u>. Form the first floor of timber all as indicated on the drawings, the joists carried on approved sheradized joist hangers built into walls. Finish floor with vinyl tiles as specified before on 3.5 mm hardboard securely pinned or stapled to the boarding at 150 mm centres overall.

4.08 <u>Roof</u>. Form the roof to the extension all as indicated on the drawings, including cutting away for as required for new wall plate on existing walls, bedding plates level and parallel, cutting and notching joists over plates to correct level for roof finish to line through, well spiking down and splay cutting, and fixing all necessary 25 mm finish distance pieces for and including 225 x 25 mm wrot deal fascia and bargeboard to whole of new and existing work to north elevation. Mix in and make out in new Welsh blue slates to line through and match existing. Each slate to be fixed with 2 no. composition or copper nails.

4.09   Gutters. Provide and fix to north elevation a new grey PVC gutter complete with 3 no. stop ends, 1 no. outlet and 2 no. angles, and all necessary fixing brackets at 3'0" centres. The gutter from the upper level is to be set across the bargeboard and left open ended to discharge on to the new roof. Take from store and refix existing r.w.p. hopper head and waste pipe to discharge into new gully.

4.10   Plastering. The plaster finishes to new walls and ceilings to be as follows:

(i)   *Ceiling to roof* – provide and fix between joists (85) mm fibreglass quilting, line soffit with 9.5 mm foil-backed plaster lath and set 5 mm Thistleboard finish to BS 1191, Pt 1: 1973 Class B.

(ii)   *Ceiling to ground floor* – line with 12.7 mm plaster lath and set 5 mm Thistleboard finish.

(iii)   *Walls* – prepare, dub out where required, render out in 1:2:9 cement/lime/sand 11 mm thick and finish with 3 mm neat anhydrous gypsum plaster to BS 1191, Pt 1: 1973 Class C.

4.11   Glazed tiling. Provide and fix three courses 150 x 150 approved white glazed tiles with bullnose free edges and pointed in white cement to back and both return ends of bath. Carry out all cutting and fitting required.

4.12   Skirting. Provide and fix 70 x 20 wrot deal standard stock skirting to BS 584: 1967 Ref. 20 RS 70 to perimeter of rooms.

4.13   Linen cupboard. Form linen cupboard with 75 x 50 fir studding, finished both sides with 9.5 mm plasterboard and skim coat plaster. Provide and fix 25 mm wrot softwood lining with 12 mm planted stop and 70 x 20 wrot standard stock architraves to BS 584: 1967 Ref. 20 RA 70, and 762 x 1981 x 35 standard hardboard faced door D15 to BS 459, Pt 2: 1962 hung on 1 no. pair 75 mm sheradized steel butt hinges. Provide to interior of cupboard 3 no. 50 x 19 wrot softwood slatted shelves on ditto bearers screwed to walls.

4.14   Doors

(i)   D6. Provide and fix to existing opening a new lining, stops and architraves and hardboard door to the opening all as specified for Door D15 above.

(ii)   D16 and D17. Provide and fix to new opening new lining, stops and architraves complete with new hardboard doors all as specified for Door D15 above.

4.15   Sanitary fittings. Include the PC Sum of £   for the supply and delivery to site of sanitary fittings by a supplier nominated by the architect as follows:

> 2 no. 1700 mm white p.e. cast iron baths, complete with hardboard side panels, pair CP taps, overflow, outlet, plug and chain.
>
> 2 no. 500 x 465 white vitreous china pedestal basins, pair CP taps, combined overflow and outlet, plug and chain.
>
> 2 no. low level white vitreous china WC suites complete with plastic seat and cover, plastic cistern, waste pipe and cone connector.

4.16   Add for profit, unloading, storing, moving to position and fixing complete (including rough framing for bath panels) and protection.

4.17   Soil and vent pipes. Provide and fix in position shown on drawings 100 mm cast-iron LCC pattern S & VP to BS 416: 1973, set to ventilate above roof and complete with Code 4 lead soaker flange and tail burnt on to iron and galvanized wire balloon guard, and cast-iron easy bend at foot with connector to stoneware. Provide and insert combination lengths comprising 100 mm branch for WC complete with 1 no. 38 mm and 1 no. 32 mm boss at first-floor level and ditto with 1 no. 38 mm and 1 no. 32 mm boss at ground-floor level.

4.18   Bracket round S & VPs with 38 x 38 fir and finish with 19 mm plasterboard lath with 5 mm skim coat gypsum plaster.

4.19   Vent pipe. Provide and fix where shown 100 mm approved grey PVC vent pipe to BS 4514: 1969 complete with offset and guard at head, and connect to drain at foot.

4.20   Traps and wastes. Traps and wastes will be in polypropylene as approved by the local authority and assembled and fixed in accordance with the manufacturer's instructions. Include for all plastic to iron connectors. Provide wastes and traps as follows:

Baths — 38 mm diameter with 75 mm deep seal
Basins — 32 mm ditto

4.21   Overflows. Provide and fix to each w.w.p. 20 mm plastic overflow pipe and splay cut and set to discharge to open air.

4.22   Ironmongery. Include the Prime Cost Sum of £   for the supply and delivery to site of ironmongery by a supplier to be nominated by the architect. Add for profit, sorting and fixing the following items:

Door D6   — 1 no. set s.a.a knob furniture
                  1 no. mortise two-lever latch
                  1 no. s.a.a. stile bolt
Door D15   — 1 no. s.a.a. 100 mm pull handle
                  1 no. 15 mm ball catch
Door D16   — 1 no. set s.a.a. knob furniture
                  1 no. mortise two-lever latch
                  1 no. s.a.a. stile bolt
Door D17   — Ditto as D16

4.23 All ironmongery to be fixed with matching screws and locks and latches adjusted and lightly oiled on completion.

5.00 ALTERATIONS TO FORM NEW SELF-CONTAINED GROUND-FLOOR FLAT AND NEW ENTRANCE

5.01 Bedroom. Remove existing fireplace and mantel complete, cut indents, sweep flue, seal opening in 75 mm block complete with opening and flue formed for and including 225 x 75 fibrous plaster vent above skirting level. Make out plaster and skirting complete.

5.02 Kitchen. Remove existing gas fire and set aside on site for re-use. Cut out and make good wall to 2 no. 225 x 150 airbricks. Remove existing sink and cupboard under, remove cupboards in recesses, demolish existing chimney breast complete including cutting back to allow for dubbing out plaster to new wall face and flue parging to obviate future sulphate attack and dub out wall. Include for hacking existing plaster as required and rendering and set to whole of wall face. Remove existing matchboard dado complete and make out plaster. Remove existing plastic tiles from ceiling and prepare for new lath. Remove existing linoleum from floor. Take down and set aside for further instructions water heater and gas cooker. Clear and cart away from site all debris.

5.03 New door D13 and frame. Needle, prop and strut as required, break through existing one-brick-thick external wall and form new opening. Rebuild reveals externally in bricks salvaged from demolition to match surrounding work, rough cut reveals internally to receive plaster, provide and build in over opening 2 no. 50 x 6 wrot iron arch bars.

5.04 Provide and fix to new opening with 6 no. sheradized cramps 100 x 50 wrot, rebated and rounded deal frame, grooved for plaster with 175 x 65 wrot, rebated and weathered hardwood sill complete with 25 x 3 galvanized water bar let into rebate.

5.05 Provide and hang to frame on 1½ pairs 100 mm steel butts 838 x 1981 x 44 wrot deal door, open and divided into a single light and glazed with broad reeded glass in putty, with internal softwood pinned beads, the door provided with hardwood weatherboard to bottom rail. Make out floor through new opening.

5.06 Linen cupboard and larder. Cut away for, block bond and form new walls of 75 mm block on 75 x 50 fir plate with 150 x 75 lintel of concrete Mix C reinforced 1 no. 10 m.s. bar over doors. Render and set walls in Sirapite.

5.07 Cut through external wall, provide and insert 225 x 225 yellow precast concrete airbricks, render flues in cement and sand and provide and fix fibrous plaster vents internally complete with flyproof gauze.

5.08 Provide and fix 25 mm wrot deal lining with 12 mm stops to openings complete with standard stock deal architraves, as described before. Provide and hang to each lining on pair of 75 mm steel butts 686 x 1981 x 35 standard stock hardboard door, all as before described.

5.09   Provide and fix in larder full length and depth 19 mm blockboard shelf (free edge lipped where exposed) and 225 mm wide shelf of 25 mm softwood on 50 x 19 wrot softwood bearers plugged and screwed to wall. Provide and fix in larder 3 no. 50 x 19 wrot softwood slatted shelves on ditto bearers plugged and screwed to wall.

5.10   Kitchen fittings. Include the PC Sum of £_____ for kitchen fittings complete with sink and drainer supplied and delivered to site by a supplier nominated by the architect. Add for profit, unloading, storing, moving to position, fixing complete and protecting as follows:

1 no. 1000 x 600 sink unit complete with s.s. sink top, taps, outlet, plug and chain; 1 no. 1000 x 600 cupboard unit complete with plastic worktop.

Provide and fix 1 course w.g. tiles to brickwork at back of sink drainer and worktop, finish with bullnose on free edges and pointed in white grout, including all cutting and fitting.

5.11   Trap and waste. Provide and fix 38 mm bottle trap and waste set to discharge under grating of new gully all as specified for bathrooms. Include for all cutting away and making good.

5.12   Skirting. Provide and fix to perimeter of kitchen, airing cupboard and larder standard stock deal skirting as described before.

5.13   Living room. Remove door D2 complete and make good to frame as required. Cut away existing defective sill and bottom of frame as required and piece in new to match in hardwood set on strip of Hyload d.p.c. Provide and hang to existing frame on 1½ pairs 100 mm steel butts a new wrot deal door open and divided into one light, all as specified for door D3 but glazed in clear sheet glass.

5.14   Floor. Take up floorboarding as necessary next partition to hall, provide and insert sawn fir to level up joists under and refix existing boarding complete. Provide and lay to floor 3 mm hardboard fixed at 150 mm centres to boarding under including all cutting and waste.

5.15   Hall. Carefully remove 2 no. existing doors and linings complete, fill in openings with 150 x 50 fir studding, face both sides with plasterboard to level up to existing plaster face and make out skirting, clear and cart away all debris.

5.16   Form 2 no. new openings in stud partitions for doors D5 and D7, trim round in 75 x 50 fir studding to form opening. Provide and fix to openings linings, stops, architraves and doors all as for doors D8 and D9. Make out floor through new openings and skirting to match existing and make good to plaster. Clear and cart away all debris.

5.17 Make out floor. Remove existing cupboard door, frame and matchboard spandrel under stairs and make out floor as shown on drawings.

5.18 Provide all necessary fir bracketing, line the underside of the staircase with 9.5 mm plasterboard lath and set gypsum plaster. Line the soffit of the half landing, short flight to upper-floor level and the whole of the ceiling to hall and entrance as above including cutting away ceiling rose and setting in 5 mm gypsum plaster as before.

5.19 Partition to stairs. Remove existing newel, balusters and handrail to bottom flight and set aside carefully for re-use as required. Form new partitions to stairs 75 x 50 fir notched over string to pass on either side to tread and soffit of string. Fill in over opening for door D4 face up both sides with 2 no. layers of 9.5 mm plasterboard lath and set in 5 mm gypsum plaster.

5.20 Provide and fix to opening 100 x 50 wrot deal frame with 25 mm rebates and standard stock architraves, both sides. Provide and hang to opening half-hour fire-resisting door to BS 459, Pt 3: 1951 to suit opening size on 1½ pairs 100 mm steel butts.

5.21 Fire protection. Remove existing dado complete and line the existing stud partition walls of the common entrance and staircase with 9.5 mm plasterboard lath (feather edge) and fill and tape and prepare for decoration.

5.22 Landing window. Remove existing landing window complete, cut back nosing to landing to original WC, form indents as required and block up opening in a one-brick wall in compo mortar and make out plaster to match existing. Clear and cart away all debris.

5.23 Floor. Repair floor in hall and entrance next partition all as specified before.

5.24 Provide and lay over existing boarding to hall, entrance, half landing and top landing 3.5 mm hardboard flooring as before.

5.25 Door D1. Remove existing door complete and clear away. Make good as required and provide and hang to frame new door to suit all as specified for door D3.

5.26 Ironmongery. Include the PC Sum of £_____ for the supply and delivery to site of ironmongery, by a supplier to be nominated by the architect. Add for profit, sorting and fixing the following items:

        D4 — 1 no. approved s.a.a. pneumatic overhead door closer
                1 no. set s.a.a. knob furniture
                1 no. 3-lever mortise lock (one escutcheon)
                1 no. s.a.a. rim cylinder night latch
                1 no. s.a.a. letter plate opening, size 200 x 44
                1 no. white plastic numeral '1'

D5 — 1 no. s.a.a. knob set
1 no. mortise latch

D7 — ditto as D5

D8 — 1 no. s.a.a. 100 mm pull handle
1 no. ball catch

D9 — ditto as D8

D1 — 1 no. set s.a.a. knob furniture
1 no. mortise latch
1 no. Chubb mortise dead lock

D2 — 1 no. set s.a.a. knob furniture
1 no. 2-lever mortise lock
2 no. mortise barrel bolts

D3 — ditto as D2

6.00   ALTERATIONS TO FORM NEW SELF-CONTAINED FIRST-FLOOR FLAT

6.01   <u>Hall</u>. Carefully demolish existing partition complete with door and frame and shelving, cut away balustrade and balusters as required for new partition, check over, remove defective remaining balusters and make good with those set aside and prepare for new partitions.

6.02   <u>New doorways</u>. Remove 2 no. doors and linings complete and make out as specified previously for lower floor. Form 2 no. new openings in stud partition for doors D12 and D13. Provide and fix doors complete all as for doors D8 and D9 (but doors to 762 mm wide) and make out to match existing.

6.03   Clear and cart away all debris.

6.04   <u>New partitions</u>. Open up existing floor, cut away for and insert new trimmer and form splayed soffit to new cupboard including making out well apron to suit.

6.05   Form new partitions all as specified for partition to stairs of studding faced with 9.5 mm plasterboard lath and set with 5 mm gypsum plaster. Provide and fix new door, linings, etc., as specified for doors D8 and D9 to new door D11 but door to be 762 mm wide. Provide and fix new full depth 19 mm blockboard shelf with lipped front edge carried on 50 x 19 wrot softwood bearers at low level in cupboard and 300 mm wide ditto at high level.

6.06   Provide and fix new half-hour fire-resisting door complete with frame all as previously specified for door D4 except that new door D10 is to be provided with an open light glazed with 6 mm Georgian wired cast glass size 450 mm square in centre at top.

6.07   Bedroom. Take out existing fireplace and gas fire complete and refix in new lounge. Cut indents, sweep flue, seal opening in 3 in. block complete with 225 x 75 f.p. vent above skirting level and make out plaster and skirting complete. Clear and cart away debris.

6.08   Lounge. Take out existing fireplace and prepare to receive that from bedroom. Sweep flue and make good and make out to match existing. Clear and cart away debris.

6.09   New opening. Form new opening through brick partition wall for door D14 generally all as specified previously for door D3. Provide and fix to new opening new linings, architraves and door complete as specified for doors D12 and D13. Make out skirting, including cutting and fitting.

6.10   Make out floor through opening with projecting nosing into kitchen and 19 mm wrot softwood riser. Form new quarter landing of 150 x 38 fir faced with 25 mm t. & g. boarding with nosing and riser to free edge and complete with skirting as specified generally.

6.11   Kitchen. Strip out existing bath, sink and brick piers, shelving, water heater and gas cooker, and gas fire. Set aside heater, cooker and fire on site and clear and cart away rest.

6.12   Cut out and make good wall to existing airbrick, demolish existing chimney breast complete all as specified for kitchen below. Hack and render and set to wall complete as specified before. Remove existing lino floor and clear and cart away all debris.

6.13   New larder. Cut away for, block bond and form new 75 mm block walls for new larder on 75 x 50 fir plate complete, with new door and lining, plaster and airbricks all as specified before. Provide 2 no. 19 mm blockboard shelves as specified before to either side of door and 2 no. 200 x 25 wrot softwood ditto full length along back door on bearers as specified

6.14   Take out existing door and frame complete and make out plaster through opening.

6.15   Kitchen fittings. Include the PC Sum of £_____ for kitchen fittings complete with sink and drainer supplied to site by a supplier to be nominated by the architect. Add for profit, unloading, storing, moving to position, fixing complete and protection as follows:

   1 no. 1000 x 600 sink unit complete with stainless steel sink top, taps, outlet, plug and chain;
   1 no. 1000 x 600 cupboard unit complete with 1500 extended plastic worktop cover.

Provide and fix to back of sink unit and worktop one course w.g. tiles finished with bullnose on free edges and pointed in white cement including all cutting and fitting.

6.16   Provide trap and waste as specified for kitchen in flat below as specified before, but set to discharge into hopper head.

6.17   <u>Water closet</u>. Remove existing window complete, draw toothings and block opening in one brick wall in stock brickwork to match existing. Remove existing door and frame complete, strip out polystyrene tiles, make out opening in 75 mm blockwork on 75 x 50 fir plate and render and set in plaster as before. Needle, prop and strut as required, cut away for and insert 2 no. new 225 x 112 lintels of concrete Mix B, each reinforced 1 no. 16 mm m.s. bar, lintels to have 150 mm bearing at each end, to form new opening for doors D16 and D17. Pin up over in slate in cement mortar. Break out brickwork face up reveals for new linings, make out floor through openings and clear and cart away all debris.

6.18   Break through existing wall and form new opening for window W3. Provide and build up reveals in stocks re-used from demolition, provide and insert to opening M4 steel light 5V2 to BS 990, Pt 2: 1972 and sill externally as specified before. Make out plaster through reveal including two coats of cold bitumen on brickwork to reveals, head and sill, and provide w.g. tile sill as before described.

6.19   <u>Ironmongery</u>. Include the PC Sum of £＿＿＿＿＿＿ for the supply and delivery to site of ironmongery, by a supplier to be nominated by the architect. Add for profit, sorting and fixing the following items:

D10   1 no. approved s.a.a. pneumatic overhead door closer
      1 no. set s.a.a. knob furniture
      1 no. 3-lever mortise lock (one escutcheon)
      1 no. s.a.a. rim cylinder night latch
      1 no. s.a.a. letter plate opening size 200 x 44
      1 no. white plastic numeral '2'

D11   1 no. s.a.a. 100 mm pull handle

D12   1 no. set s.a.a. knob furniture
      1 no. mortise latch

D13   Ditto as D12

D14   Ditto as D12

D18   1 no. 100 mm pull handle
      1 no. ball catch

7.00   ELECTRICAL INSTALLATION

7.01   Installation. Include the Prime Cost Sum of £ _____ for the electrical installation complete, the work to be carried out by a subcontractor nominated by the architect.

7.02   Add for profit and attendance including all chasing, drilling and cutting away in connection with the following points (provisional):

13 no. ceiling lighting points
14 no. 13 A power points
 2 no. cooker control units
 2 no. bell installations
 2 no. immersion heater control points
 2 no. TV jack outlets
 1 no. night storage heater outlet

7.03   Service cable. Include the Provisional Sum of £ _____ for alterations and additions to the electric service cables to provide for separate service to each flat.

7.04   The contractor is to allow in his tender for the following work (provisional):

(a)   Covering up and protecting existing night storage heater and moving as required to facilitate works and placing in position under stairs on completion;

(b)   Breaking through foundations and inserting 2 no. 100 mm s.g.s. easy bends into meter cupboard for new cable intake and make good.

(c)   Shut off existing power supply and strip out the whole of the existing installation complete and make good where exposed.

7.05   Clear and cart away from site all debris.

8.00   PLUMBING AND HEATING INSTALLATION

8.01   Gas installation. Make arrangements with the gas board to disconnect the gas service at its entry into the building and blank off temporarily and remove the meter.

8.02   Strip out the whole of the existing gas installation complete, make good where disturbed and clear and cart away from site.

8.03   Include the Provisional Sum of £ _____ for the following work to be carried out by the gas board.

(a)   Ground floor flat. Break into existing main in road, run supply into building terminating in isolator and meter in cupboard at side of front door. Run gas supply below floor to cooker position in kitchen and to gas fire (re-used) in living room complete with control valve and connect to gas fire.

(b)   <u>First floor flat</u>. Connect to existing main supply and run service into meter cupboard as above at high level terminating in isolator and meter. Run gas supply through floor above to cooker position in kitchen and to gas fire in living room complete with control valve and connect to gas fire.

8.04   <u>Main water service installation</u>. Strip out the whole of the plumbing installation above the main stopcock and clear and cart away from site.

8.05   Break through existing ceiling over top landing of stairs and form new ceiling trap hatch of size to take new cisterns, trim round opening with 100 x 50 fir, provide and fix new 19 mm wrot softwood lining with 19 mm planted stop and standard architrave complete with 19 mm blockboard loose cover. Seal off existing hatch by removing cover and lining and making out, and setting in gypsum plaster. Line the underside of the hatch with 9.5 mm plasterboard. Provide and fix across stairwell 3 no. 150 x 50 fir bearers with 12 mm chipboard to support storage cistern.

8.06   Provide and install in roof 2 no. 227-litre polyolefin cisterns to BS 4213: 1975 inter-connected to provide water board's storage requirements complete with approved BS ball valve with plastic float. Make connection with existing supply under ground floor with new 15 mm brass combined stop and drain cock in bottom of meter cupboard and raise service into roof space in floor and cupboards and connect to ball valve. Run 15 mm services to sink positions with stop valve under each sink and connect to sink top.

8.07   <u>Cold water down service</u>. Make 2 no. 22 mm connections to storage cisterns and drop cold water down services through linen cupboard of upper flat. Provide in cupboard a stop valve for upper flat and run 22 mm service to bath tap with 15 mm branches to basin and WC w.w.p. Continue service to lower flat to floor level, with stop valve under WC and run 22 mm services to bath with 15 mm branches to basin tap and WC w.w.p.

8.08   Make connection to storage cistern and run 2 no. 28 mm supplies and connect to cylinder complete with stop valves in linen cupboards.

8.09   <u>Hot water service</u>. Provide and install in linen cupboards 2 no. 114-litre direct copper cylinders each complete with 3 kW electric immersion heater with switch complete with neon light. The cylinders to be set on hardwood blocks for bottom ventilation. Run 22 mm service to bathroom and connect to bath tap with 15 mm services to sink and basin, with 15 mm expansion pipe set to discharge over storage cisterns in roof space. Provide 15 mm draw off cock at lowest point of each installation for draining down.

8.10   <u>Lagging</u>. Lag all pipes in floors and roof spaces with (25) mm fibreglass lagging well wired on. Provide to storage cisterns 12 mm insulation board boxing screwed to fir corner bearers and cross-bracketing and fill void with loose exfoliated mica fill with 12 mm polystyrene cover. Provide and fix to cylinders approved fibreglass lagging jacket with glazed cover.

9.00   GENERAL REPAIRS TO PROPERTY

9.01   <u>External.</u> All work specified is to include for making out and making good to match surrounding work and for clearing and carting away all debris.

9.02   <u>Works to roof.</u> Take off existing ridge tiles and rebed and repoint in cement and sand (1:3).

9.03   Hack off all loose and defective verge fillets and re-run as required. Take off verge tiles as required, reset and nail and rebed in cement and sand to fall inwards from verge.

9.04   Carefully demolish 3 no. chimney stacks to below roof level (in 1 no.) or to 150 mm above roof pitch. Make out roof over 1 no. stack to match existing. Remove slates as required, provide and insert new Code 4 lead soakers, rebuild 2 no. stacks to match existing complete with new Code 4 lead safes, stepped flashings and front aprons and 4 no. new red terracotta pots well flaunched up in cement and sand (1:3).

9.05   Carefully overhaul existing roof slopes, renew all missing or cracked slates to match existing. Overhaul roof to bay window including checking and re-bedding hip slates as necessary and making out where water heater flue removed.

9.06   Provide and line the underside of the existing rafters to the main roof slope with foil backed sarking felt.

9.07   Clean out existing gutters and r.w.p.s, remove all rust, check and remake all leaking joints, paint insides of gutters one coat of Rustodian and two coats black bitumastic paint.

9.08   <u>Works to existing external walls.</u> Cut out and make good cracks in face brickwork as follows:

(a)   over bay window roof
(b)   to both sides of bay window
(c)   to brickwork under bay window sill
(d)   over arch to front entrance door
(e)   repair sill to small window over front entrance door
(f)   crack between sill and head of window on front elevation
(g)   Repair slipped arch at eaves level over kitchen window and crack between sill and window head below
(h)   Repair sill to ground floor kitchen window
(j)   Cut out and make good air brick under sill to new door D3
       Cut away for, provide and build 2 no. new air bricks 225 x 75 to ventilate floor under kitchen

9.09   Brush down and treat whole of existing face brickwork with two coats of approved silicone waterproofer.

9.10   Works to existing windows. Carefully repair existing windows as follows:

(a)   Ground floor bedroom. Renew 2 no. rotten bottom sashes, parting beads and sash cords complete including glass to match, re-using fastenings.

(b)   Ground floor living room. Renew 2 no. rotten bottom sashes in bay window with glass and sash cords complete, re-using fastenings.

(c)   Ground floor kitchen. Renew rotten bottom sash, glass, parting beads and sash cords complete, re-using fastenings.

(d)   First floor hall. Renew bottom rotten sash, parting beads, glass and sash cords complete, re-using fastenings.

(e)   First floor bedroom. Renew 3 no. rotten bottom sashes in window over bay with parting beads, glass and sash cords complete, re-using fastenings.

(f)   Renew pane of glass over ground floor living room door.

9.11   Woodworm infestation. Include the Prime Cost Sum of £ _____ for treatment of the property against beetle infestation by a specialist subcontractor to be appointed by the architect. Add for profit and attendance.

9.12   Rising damp. Include the Provisional Sum of £ _____ for treatment against rising damp.

9.13   Treatment against damp walls. Carefully remove picture rails, skirtings, etc., and set aside for re-use. Strip off wallpaper where found, hack plaster off wall, clean down, provide and fix from floor level to ceiling Newtonite lath all in accordance with the manufacturer's instructions. Render and set in plaster as described before. Re-fix skirtings and picture rails and make good all work disturbed. This work is to be carried out to the following areas:

(a)   Ground floor living room to external walls *except* for chimney breast
(b)   Ground floor bedroom to south and east external walls *except* for chimney breast
(c)   Ground floor kitchen to east and north walls, taking into account new work and new door opening

9.14   Cracks. Cut out all cracks in the plaster of the property and refill and make good incorporating plasterer's scrim.

10.00   PAINTING AND DECORATION

10.01   External woodwork

(a)   *New* – knot, prime with wood primer no. 2, stop and paint one undercoat and two coats gloss.
(b)   *Existing* – burn off all loose, crazed or defective paintwork, prepare prime one coat wood primer no. 2 to bare spots, bring forward and paint one undercoat and two coats gloss.

10.02   <u>Internal woodwork</u>

(a)   *New* – knot, prime, stop and paint one undercoat and one coat gloss.

(b)   *Existing* – wash off well and rub down to remove loose or crazed paint, touch up bare wood with wood primer no. 2, bring forward and paint one undercoat and one coat gloss.

10.03   <u>Ferrous metalwork</u>. Rub down and wire brush to remove all rust, paint one coat Billingham chromate primer, one coat undercoat and two coats gloss.

10.04   <u>Ceilings</u>. Strip where papered, rub down all ceilings, wash off existing, fill all shrinkage cracks, prepare, line with good-quality lining paper and paint two coats emulsion.

10.05   <u>Walls</u>. Generally strip off all wallpaper to existing walls, wash down and prepare all walls for lining or papering as follows:

(a)   Entrance hall and staircase – paper with Vymura paper PC Sum of £   per piece.

(b)   Kitchens, bathrooms and WC – paper with washable paper PC Sum of £   per piece.

(c)   Remainder of walls to be lined with good quality lining paper and finished two coats emulsion.

10.06   <u>External window sills, etc</u>. Window sills and bay window to have all loose paintwork scraped off, bare areas and new rendering painted two coats alkali-resisting primer and the whole painted one undercoat and two coats gloss.

11.00   DRAINAGE AND EXTERNAL WORKS

11.01   <u>Pipes and fittings</u>. Pipes and fittings will be (BS quality s.g.s or such quality as may be approved by the local authority).

11.02   Remove existing concrete cover to manhole, seal off branch to external WC, break through walls and benching and insert two new branches and make good all work disturbed including existing rendering. Provide and bed new single-seal cast-iron frame to manhole complete with cover set in grease after painting both two coats of black bitumastic paint.

11.03   Excavate on line of existing common drain, locate and open up and form new manhole of size shown on drawing and as specified. Break into drain and insert new brownware channel with branch and provide and bed as specified above new 610 x 457 single-seal cast-iron cover and frame to manhole.

11.04   Excavate for and build new manhole where shown on drawing all as specified before.

11.05   Provide and set new 225 x 225 gully with precast concrete kerb, 100 mm back inlet with knuckle to receive 75 mm waste pipe and black cast-iron-grating perforated to receive kitchen sink waste. Render back brickwork 25 mm thick in cement and sand (1:3).

11.06   Provide, excavate for to even falls and gradients and lay s.g.s. foul drains to lines shown all as specified on 100 mm concrete Mix A and flaunched up after testing. Return fill-in and consolidate excavated material around pipes and break in tops of trenches for three times their width under all pavings. Clear and cart away all surplus and debris.

11.07   Existing WC, etc. Carefully demolish existing external WC and fuel store complete, grub out foundations and backfill with excavated material, grub out drains and well sprinkle out trenches with lime. Make good all to match existing, including cleaning down exterior walls to remove lime whitening.

11.08   Form new step to door D3 of fine concrete Mix C set on bed of hardcore 100 mm thick, finished smooth on all exposed faces.

11.09   New paving. Break out old existing paving, excavate for as required and lay 100 mm of concrete Mix D (or brick hardcore if available) set to falls away from the building. Provide and bed 450 × 450 × 38 approved grey precast concrete paving in cement and sand (1:4) and recess point in same material. Clear and cart away all surplus excavated material. Carry out all cutting and fitting required.

Schedule of Prime Cost and Provisional Sums	2.00	Provisional Sum of £ . . . for contingencies
	4.15	Prime Cost Sum of £ . . . for sanitary fittings
	4.22	Prime Cost Sum of £ . . . for ironmongery to new extension
	5.10	Prime Cost Sum of £ . . . for kitchen fittings for ground floor flat
	5.26	Prime Cost Sum of £ . . . for ironmongery for ground floor flat
	6.15	Prime Cost Sum of £ . . . for kitchen fittings for first floor flat
	6.19	Prime Cost Sum of £ . . . for ironmongery for first floor flat
	7.01	Prime Cost Sum of £ . . . for electrical installation
	7.03	Provisional Sum of £ . . . for electric service cables
	8.03	Provisional Sum of £ . . . for gas installation
	9.11	Prime Cost Sum of £ . . . for treatment against beetle infestation
	9.12	Provisional Sum of £ . . . for treatment against rising damp
	10.05	Prime Cost Sum of £ . . . per piece for wallpaper in entrance hall and staircase
		Prime Cost Sum of £ . . . per piece for wallpaper in kitchens, bathrooms and WC

11 Specifications and layout for improvement grant work

Building works carried out with the help of improvement grants or by means of Housing Corporation finance through a local authority are best set out in such a way that the estimator can break down his tender into 'improvements' and 'repairs'.

To both assist the estimator and architect, and to provide an immediate breakdown of the tender into the two separate sections, all specifications for this type of work should have cash columns against those clauses with a precise financial bearing on the tender. In general, this affects the sections of the specifications covering the preliminaries as well as the specific work clauses. (Workmanship and material clauses are not affected, as they are descriptive: they refer only to qualities or general matters in the individual work clauses.) In addition, it is advisable to assist the estimator, by indicating whether an item is a 'repair' or 'maintenance', that is, by setting against each item either 'R' for repairs or 'I' for improvements. In pricing the preliminaries, the contractor will, in most cases, apportion his overheads and profit, etc., proportionally between the cost of repairs and maintenance unless he includes for such costs in each work item priced.

Directions in respect of the form of contract will be issued by the architect. However, the specification writer should bear in mind that while the Agreement for Minor Building Works is generally suitable for this type of work, work carried out with Housing Corporation finance should be under the Standard Form of Building Contract, Without Quantities.

Prime Cost and Provisional Sums generally should be omitted and the works specified out in full. This will mean the prior selection of sanitary fittings, floor finishes, etc., so that the contractor can include in his estimate for the items selected. The only Provisional Sum that should be included is one for contingencies, to cover repair works unforeseen when the works were specified or that come to light during the course of the works. Where the work is of a highly specialized nature, such as the insertion of a new damp-proof course, then a Prime Cost Sum for the work can be inserted.

The first section of the specification, therefore, will incorporate the general contract and preliminary clauses as described in Chapter 7, but with the addition of double cash columns; this is illustrated in specific examples below. Monetary items need not be separated into 'Improvements' or 'Repairs', as in most cases the cost of complying with these clauses will be expressed either as a lump sum carried to the collection or as a percentage added to the net cost of each work item. Care must be taken to select only those alternative clauses applicable to contracts of this nature (see Chapter 7), and to close the cash columns after the final clause dealing with preliminaries for transfer to the collection page at the end of the specification.

The following example is part of a larger specification dealing with a small contract for alterations, improvements and repairs to a property, finance for which is to come from an improvement grant. The example, together with the preliminaries given in Chapter 7 and the material and workmanship clauses described in Chapter 10, illustrates a method for dealing with this type of work by the layout suggested.

		Improve-ments		Repairs, etc.	
		£	p	£	p
	SECTION 3 *The works*				
4.01	<u>Scope of works</u>. The works comprise improvements and repairs to an existing two-storey terraced house for use as a five-person, family unit.				
	Items marke (I) and (R), i.e. 'Improvements' and 'Repairs' are to be priced in the corresponding cash columns. Such symbols shall apply to all items immediately above, unless otherwise indicated.				
4.02	<u>Generally</u>. Clear away rubbish from garden and within the building. (R)				
	Strip out all existing sanitary fittings, ranges, etc., through-out, unless otherwise described, and cart away. Allow Credit hereafter. (I)				
	Strip out all visible pipes and cut off under floors and behind plaster and make good finishings. (I)				
	Strip all floor coverings on first floor, draw all nails and clean off boards. (I)				
	Sweep all flues throughout and cart soot from site. (R)				
	Remove fireplaces or shutting-in boards from all rooms (except in back addition), take up hearths and seal up openings in 75 mm blockwork. (I)				
	Overhaul all deal-cased frames and sashes not affected by works described hereafter, renew all cords, cut out and renew perished putties, oil and adjust ironmongery (re-placing where missing or damaged), ease sashes, balance and leave in working order. (R)				
4.03	<u>Demolitions</u>. Break up benching around external WC and make out floor and wall face. (I)				
	Cut away brickwork in 500 mm deep chimney breast on both floors of back addition and in roof space over, to leave a one-brick projection, clean out exposed flues and brick up and remove hearth. (Projection of stack over is 225 mm.) (I)				
	To collection £					

	Improve-ments		Repairs, etc.	
	£	p	£	p

Take down 75 mm solid cross partition in kitchen, including door and linings.   (I)

Take down 75 mm solid partition between front and rear living rooms and temporarily support work above.   (I)

Take down all 75 mm solid partitions on first floor rear addition including partition behind staircase landing and two doors and linings.   (I)

Take down two-courses high brick walling around front garden, prepare and build new half-brick wall 800 mm high in stock facings jointed both sides and with brick-on-end coping. Build similar separating wall between gardens on either side.   (I)

4.39   Clothes post. Provide rotary clothes post in back garden set in 225 mm concrete base let in flush with ground with a metal sleeve mortised in.   (I)

4.40   Decorations. Rub down, bring forward and paint two undercoats and one gloss finish on eaves fascias and soffits, and all other existing paintwork to front and rear.   (R)

Knot, prime, stop and paint three undercoats and one gloss finish on new window and door joinery, fascias, soffits, etc.   (I)

4.41   Gardens. Cut down overgrowth in rear garden.   (R)

Cut down bushes and saplings in rear garden.   (R)

4.42   Garden Store. Take out door and frame from former external WC, construct new 44 mm framed, ledged and braced door covered with 25 mm t. & g. boarding and 88 × 63 rebated frame and fix in opening size 710 × 1820.   (R)

4.43   Leave in good order. Leave the whole of the property clean, free from builder's rubbish and in good working order, and test all services to the satisfaction of the respective authorities.   (I)

To collection   £

	Improve-ments		Repairs, etc.	
	£	p	£	p

CREDITS

Credit all marketable materials arising from demolitions
works described herein including one gas cooker.   (I)

To collection   £

COLLECTIONS

Page   1
     2
     3
   11
   12
   20
   21
   22

   £

      £

Less credits   £

   £   £

Total to form of tender   £

12 The National Building Specification

The National Building Specification (NBS) was first published in 1973 as a book in four volumes. At the time there were complaints about the difficulty of updating, and so in 1975 a subscription service was started. The original text was completely revised and republished in loose-leaf form in a set of six binders. Subscribers pay annually and receive revised and new sections four times a year. The NBS is published by a RIBA company, NBS Limited, and is available from NBS Services, Mansion House Chambers, The Close, Newcastle upon Tyne NE1 3RE.

The NBS is a library of specification clauses, arranged in work sections which are based on current subcontracting practice in the building industry. For example:

F21   Brick/block/stone walling
N34   Metal profiled sheet roofing/cladding
P51   Coated macadam/asphalt paving

The sections have been coded according to the CI/Sf.B classification system. However the order in which they are arranged can be varied and subscribers have a choice of the CI/Sf.B or the SMM sequence.

Also included in the subscription service is an abridged version of the text — the Small Jobs Version, intended for smaller and/or simpler projects. It comes in both arrangements and is kept up to date. It is also available for purchase as a book without updating.

An important feature of the NBS is the guidance notes. These are positioned alongside each clause on the same page and are an essential aid to the specifier when preparing a job specification. Not only do they assist in the selection and completion of clauses but they also direct the specifier to other sources of information.

The work sections are subdivided into groups of clauses for materials and workmanship. Materials may be specified either by reference to a particular maker's products or to British Standards, and are classified in groups generally to CI/Sf.B Table 2 divisions. Workmanship clauses are grouped into subsections such as 'preparation of sub-base', 'laying' and 'protection'. Each work section is designed to be read as a whole and cross-referencing to other sections is kept to a minimum.

Each section of a specification for a particular job is prepared by selecting standard clauses and inserting additional information where and as required, together with 'special' (that is, non-NBS) clauses where necessary to cover special or particular items of work. Great care must be taken to select from the very wide range of clauses offered, only those which are specifically required.

Expendable copies of NBS work sections are available for marking up. The stages for preparing a specification are:

(a) Select the relevant work section (e.g. brick/block walling).
(b) Select the materials clauses required, and insert any additional information where necessary.
(c) Delete materials clauses not required.
(d) Insert new materials clauses for special or particular items.
(e) Select related workmanship clauses to complement the materials selected.
(f) Delete workmanship clauses not required together with any alternative or conflicting clauses.

The specification is then typed and reproduced in the normal way.

The clause codes are not essential to the specification except where cross-reference is required. However, they are useful for revising NBS published texts and enable the reader to distinguish between standard clauses and special clauses.

The example on pages 144–53 shows how to prepare a work section using the Small Jobs Version of a typical NBS section. The NBS guidance notes are of great help when selecting and completing the required clauses. The typed final version of this section of the specification is shown on pages 154–5.

L23   PLASTICS/SHEET ROOF

COVERINGS is the work section title. Like many others in the NBS, it is structured to allow easy alteration for the project specification.

SCHEDULE OF TYPES OF COVERING

Schedules occur in many NBS sections, and give a useful summary of the work to be done. They act as a checklist for the specifier when preparing the specification, and give the contractor a clear picture of the different types of work required and the variations between them.

Published December 1979

For further information about built-up roofing including insulation and control of condensation see:
CP 144: Part 3, 'Roof coverings; Built-up bitumen felt'.
BRE Digest 144, 'Asphalt and built-up felt roofings: durability'.
BRE Digest 180, 'Condensation in roofs'.
BRE Digest 221, 'Flat roof design: the technical options'.
BRE Digest 224, 'Cellular plastics for building'.
Felt Roofing Contractors Advisory Board publication 'Built-up roofing'.
Architects Journal, 14 May 1975, pp 1047 – 1052, 'The inverted roof'.

SCHEDULE OF TYPES

Use this schedule item for roofs with no insulation or with the insulation applied over the weathering layer (protected membrane roofing). Complete as follows:
- Location: this sub-item will be unnecessary on small jobs
- Base: e.g. 'Galvanized steel deck'
  Primer: insert 'required' or 'not required'.
- Underlayer: e.g. 'Glass fibre base, type 3B'
  Bonding: e.g. 'full', 'partial', 'nailed', or 'not required'.
- Covering layer(s): e.g:
  'Intermediate: glass fibre based, type 3B'
  'Top: green mineral surfaced glass fibre based, type 3E'
  'Bonding: full'.
- External insulation: applicable to protected membrane roofs, e.g. '50mm Styromate 3000S'.
- Applied finish: e.g. '50mm ballast Y650'.
- Accessories: e.g. 'Edge trim X510'.

Use this schedule item for roof coverings with insulation below the weathering layer. Complete as follows:
- Location: e.g. 'Roof to changing rooms'.
- Base: e.g. 'Pre-felted woodwool slabs'.
  Primer: insert 'required' or 'not required'.
- Vapour barrier: e.g. 'asbestos based, type 2B', or 'Trucap D5'
  Bonding: e.g. 'full'.
- Insulation: e.g. '50mm pre-felted expanded polystyrene, R210 with 13mm fibreboard overlay R610'
  Bonding: e.g. 'full'.
- Covering layer(s): e.g. 'Asbestos based, type 2B'
  Bonding: e.g. 'full'.
- Applied finish: e.g. 'White spar chippings Y611'.
- Accessories: e.g. 'Edge trim X510'.

(L23) ~~PLASTICS/~~FELT SHEET ROOF COVERINGS   **L23**

To be read in conjunction with Preliminaries and
General Conditions.

SCHEDULE OF TYPES OF COVERING

~~L23/~~   Location: _ _ _ _ _ _ _ _ _ _ _ _ _ _ _ _ _

        Base: _ _ _ _ _ _ _ _ _ _ _ _ _ _ _ _ _
                           Primer: _ _ _ _ _ _ _ _ _ _ _ _ _

        Underlayer: _ _ _ _ _ _ _ _ _ _ _ _ _ _ _ _ _
                           Bonding: _ _ _ _ _ _ _ _ _ _ _ _ _

        Covering layer(s): Intermediate: _ _ _ _ _ _ _ _ _ _
                           Top: _ _ _ _ _ _ _ _ _ _ _ _ _ _ _
                           Bonding of covering layer(s): _ _ _
        External
        insulation: _ _ _ _ _ _ _ _ _ _ _ _ _ _ _ _ _

        Applied finish: _ _ _ _ _ _ _ _ _ _ _ _ _ _ _ _ _

        Accessories: _ _ _ _ _ _ _ _ _ _ _ _ _ _ _ _ _

(L23/1)   Location: *Office extension* _ _ _ _ _ _ _ _

        Base: *Pre-felted woodwool slabs* _ _ _
                           ~~Primer:~~ _ _ _ _ _ _ _ _ _ _ _ _ _

        ~~Vapour barrier:~~   _ _ _ _ _ _ _ _ _ _ _ _ _ _ _ _ _
                           ~~Bonding:~~ _ _ _ _ _ _ _ _ _ _ _ _ _

        Insulation: *Polystyrene R210 with Fibreboard R610*
                           Bonding: *full* _ _ _ _ _ _ _ _ _ _

        Covering layer(s): First: _ _ _ *Glass fibre 3B* _
                           Intermediate: _ *Glass fibre 3B* _
                           Top: _ _ _ _ *Glass fibre 3B* _
                           Bonding of covering layer(s): *full* _

        Applied finish: *Chippings* _ _ _ _ _ _ _ _ _ _ _

        Accessories: *Edge trim* _ _ _ _ _ _ _ _ _ _ _

L23   PRODUCTS/MATERIALS
Products are grouped and coded in accordance with the form of the product, for example:

A   Main product or material
R   Rigid sheets
X   Components/Accessories

Clause numbers are not consecutive, thereby allowing NBS to insert additional items at later dates, and allowing the specification writer to insert 'non-standard' items.

A210   This clause has been selected for inclusion in the project specification but the choice of manufacturer is being left to the contractor.

R210   Clauses not required are deleted.

A210
See General Guidance Notes on Page 1. 'Manufacturer and reference' can be deleted if not required.

R210, R410
The high insulation value of cellular plastics boards can cause large temperature build-up in coverings due to solar gain. Consult sheet covering manufacturer or roofing contractor.

R210
Only two grades of expanded polystyrene board are suitable for roofs, HD (high duty) and EHD (extra high duty), the latter being for areas subject to heavy pedestrian traffic.

Expanded polystyrene boards laid under the weatherproofing layer should be pre-felted to protect against mechanical damage and excessive heat from bonding compounds. Expanded polystyrene board should not be used for protected membrane roofing unless it is of extruded foam, which has a closed—cell structure making it resistant to absorption of water.

R410
Use this clause for boards of foamed polystyrene, polyurethene, polyisocyanurate, phenolic resin, foamed glass, rockwool, etc.

R610
Primarily intended as a protective overlay for cellular plastics boards with a low melting point, e.g. polystyrene.

X510
Edge trims are available in mill finish and anodized aluminium, PVC and GRP.

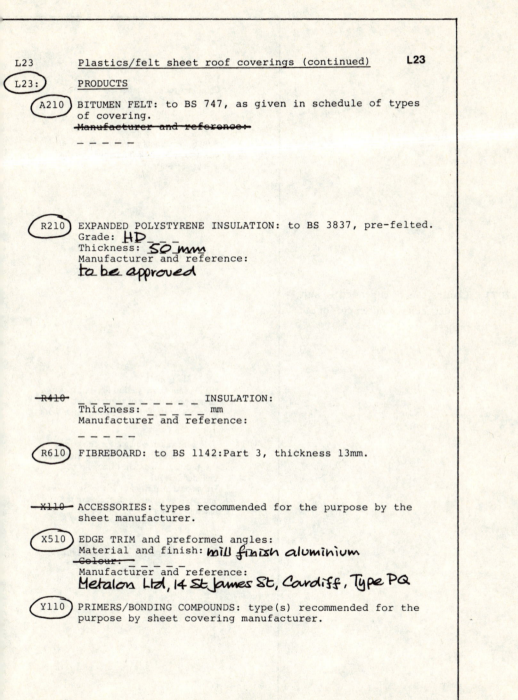

L23   Plastics/felt sheet roof coverings (continued)   **L23**

L23:   PRODUCTS

A210   BITUMEN FELT: to BS 747, as given in schedule of types
        of covering.
        ~~Manufacturer and reference:~~
        _ _ _ _ _

R210   EXPANDED POLYSTYRENE INSULATION: to BS 3837, pre-felted.
        Grade: **HD** _ _ _
        Thickness: **50 mm**
        Manufacturer and reference:
        to be approved

~~R410~~   _ _ _ _ _ _ _ _ _ _ INSULATION:
        Thickness: _ _ _ _ _ mm
        Manufacturer and reference:
        _ _ _ _ _

R610   FIBREBOARD: to BS 1142:Part 3, thickness 13mm.

~~X110~~ ACCESSORIES: types recommended for the purpose by the
        sheet manufacturer.

X510   EDGE TRIM and preformed angles:
        Material and finish: **mill finish aluminium**
        ~~Colour:~~ _ _ _ _
        Manufacturer and reference:
        Metalon Ltd, 14 St James St, Cardiff, Type PQ

Y110   PRIMERS/BONDING COMPOUNDS: type(s) recommended for the
        purpose by sheet covering manufacturer.

Y611
Chippings for solar reflective finishes.
Insert type e.g:
'hard limestone'

Y650
Rain water outlets should have a gravel
guard capable of excluding the specified
size of aggregate.

2071   Clauses can be amended to suit
the particular requirements of the
project.

2121, 2171, 2221
NBS Preliminaries section A53:4 contains a
range of definitions of terms for use in
alteration, extension and maintenance work.

2171
This is intended as a base for one or more
layers of new felt. Patching pure and simple
(i.e. producing a patched finish) is not
included in NBS.
Provisional quantities of felt to be removed
and replaced should be included in the
schedule of work.

2221
1. Insert 'chippings', 'paving tiles', etc.

L23   Plastics/felt sheet roof coverings (continued)   **L23**

(Y611)   CHIPPINGS:
         Type: hard limestone
         Size: 9 mm

~~Y650~~   BALLAST: washed round gravel, size 16-32mm, all finer
         aggregate screened off.

(L23:)   WORKMANSHIP

         GENERALLY/PREPARATION

(1301)   QUALITY OF WORK: handle, store and lay sheets and
         ancillary materials neatly to manufacturer's
         recommendations to make the whole sound and weathertight
         at the earliest opportunity before Practical Completion.
         Repair any defects as quickly as practicable to minimise
         damage and nuisance.

(2071)   SUITABILITY OF BASE: before laying coverings ensure
         that roof is to correct falls and all preliminary work
         including ~~formation of grooves, provision of battens~~
         ~~and fillets and~~ fixing of roof outlets to correct
         levels is complete. Base for sheeting must be clean and
         dry. Sub-contractor must confirm to Main Contractor and
         SO his agreement that the base is suitable.

~~2121~~   EXISTING FELT COVERINGS: the extent to which existing
         coverings are removed must be agreed with the SO before
         the work is started. Remove existing coverings in ways
         which will minimise the amount of removal and renewal.

~~2171~~   PATCHING OF EXISTING FELT as base for new felt:
         1. Remove defective felt and bonding compound where
            directed back to a sound edge.
         2. Cut back each layer at least 100mm from the layer
            below, taking care not to cut through the layer
            below.
         3. Replace with felt of equivalent material and finish,
            accurately cut to butt joint with existing felt.
            Bond each layer as adjacent existing felt.

~~2221~~   EXISTING FELT TO BE RETAINED:
         1. Remove _ _ _ _ _ _ _ _ _ _, dust, dirt and grease.
         2. Remove any moss and treat surfaces with fungicide.
         3. Cut blisters and wrinkles open and stick flaps down
            with bonding compound.
         4. Fill cracks with bitumen-based mastic and cover with
            150mm wide strip of felt bedded in mastic.
         5. Prime all surfaces to which new felt is to be bonded.

2271
To accommodate minor movement between
adjacent sheets, panels, slabs, screed bays, etc.

2501
It is not always practical to stagger the end
joints of boards which are tapered to a fall.

2551
Most cellular plastics and particularly
expanded polystyrene should be covered with
fibreboard. This provides a stable surface for
the sheet covering and protects the insulation
from mechanical damage. The fibreboard
should be included in the schedule under the
sub-item of Insulation.

2651
The use of pre-felted boards should be
considered.

3221, 3222
The lower layer of felt roofing on concrete,
screeds, particle boards, laminated boards and
asbestos surfaces should be partially bonded.
The centres of ventilation channels are
dependent on the area and shape of the roof.
Usually about 90% of the perimeter should
be bonded which would give channels at
1500mm centres.

3271
Nailing is recommended for fixing to timber
boarded surfaces, but partial bonding is
normal for plywood and chipboard bases.

Glass fibre based felt, due to its low tear-
resistance, is not suitable for nailing.
When glass fibre based felt is laid over timber
the underlayer should be an asbestos based felt.

3321A   'Special' clause inserted to cover
an aspect of workmanship pecu-
liar to the project and so not
covered by NBS.

3321A   DRESS FELT to eaves trim and seal to
aluminium. Dress felt over timber fillet
under roof tiles.

L23   <u>Plastics/felt sheet roof coverings (continued)</u>   **L23**

(2271) JOINTS IN BASE: cover with 150mm wide felt strip bonded
at edges only.

~~2451~~ VAPOUR BARRIER: lay as specified with additional
perimeter margin not less than 225mm wide. Wrap over
edge of insulation and stick down with continuous strip
of self-adhesive tape.

(2501) INSULATION: lay as specified, with staggered end joints
and all joints close-butted.

~~2502~~ INSULATION: ensure that all edges are supported by crown
of deck corrugations.

(2551) FIBREBOARD OVERLAY: fully bond to insulation by applying
hot bonding compound to fibreboard and not to insulation.
Lay with staggered, close-butted joints, to break joint
with insulation.

(2651) MOISTURE-ABSORBENT MATERIALS: lay sheets to cover dry-
laid moisture-absorbent base or insulation on the same
day as the base or insulation is laid. Seal exposed
edges of base or insulation at the end of each day's
work or at the first sign of rain.

<u>LAYING SHEETS/ACCESSORIES/FINISHES</u>

~~3221~~ PARTIAL BONDING of ordinary felt, when specified, means
spot, strip or frame bond with hot bonding compound.
Fully bond perimeter of roof for a width of 450mm
leaving 150mm wide ventilating channels at _ _ _ _ _
centres.

~~3222~~ PARTIAL BONDING of venting base layer, when specified,
means leave central area loose for later bonding by
application of compound for subsequent layer of felt.
Fully bond perimeter for 'a width of 450mm leaving 150mm
wide ventilation channels at _ _ _ _ _ mm centres.

~~3271~~ NAILING, when specified, means fix to timber boarded
base at 50mm centres at edges and laps and at 150mm
staggered centres over area of sheet.

(3321) BITUMEN FELT: lay sheets in the direction of the roof
slope with 50mm side and 75mm end laps, all fully
sealed. Break bond between layers.

5101
Skirt of copper vents normally requires
priming. See also guidance note to clause X211.

5252
A levelling sheet is required over bonded-on
aggregate finishes on existing roofs to prevent
indentation of insulation when loaded with
ballast.

5351
Insert 'roof covering' or 'insulation' or
'paving'.

5451
Suitable for felt roofing up to 10° pitch
where frequent foot traffic is not anticipated.

L23   <u>Plastics/felt sheet roof coverings (continued)</u>   **L23**

~~3322~~   BITUMEN FELT: prevent adhesion of squeezed out bonding
           compound to surface of mineral surfaced felt. Remove
           surplus.

~~3421~~   INTERNAL ANGLES which have no fillet to be reinforced
           with 100mm wide strip of felt, fully bonded.

~~3451~~   EAVES: form drip to eaves with 200mm wide strip of felt,
           nail one edge at 150mm centres, fold to form welt 50mm
           deep and seal with bonding compound. Fully bond remainder
           of felt to base and cover with full thickness of built-
           up finish.

~~3501~~   VERGES: form drip to verge with 250mm wide strip of felt,
           nail one edge at 150mm centres, fold to form welt 50mm
           deep and seal with bonding compound. Fully bond remainder
           of felt to top layer of roofing.

~~3554~~   FLASHINGS: tuck top edge into chase not less than 25mm
           deep, secure with lead wedges at 600mm centres and fully
           bond to felt upstand.

(5101)   VENTS:
           1. Position vents evenly over the roof area, one to
              every _ 4 _ m².
           2. Do not prime or apply adhesive to base below vents.
           3. Prime skirt of vents before felting if recommended
              by manufacturer.

~~5252~~   EXTERNAL INSULATION: before laying boards, cover
           existing chippings with levelling sheet.

~~5351~~   BALLAST: spread evenly to a depth of 50mm as soon as the
           _ _ _ _ _ _ _ _ _ _ has been laid.

(5451)   BONDED CHIPPINGS FINISH:
           1. Apply as soon as the roof is clear of other sub-trades.
           2. Apply bitumen dressing compound and immediately dress
              with chippings closely bedded at the rate of 16kg/m².
           3. Remove loose chippings.

The completed section typed up for inclusion in the job specification

---

L23   <u>FELT SHEET ROOF COVERINGS</u>   L23

To be read in conjunction with Preliminaries and General Conditions.

<u>SCHEDULE OF TYPES OF COVERING</u>

L23/1   Location: Office extension

Base: Pre-felted woodwool slabs

Insulation: Polystyrene R210 with Fibreboard R610
                         Bonding: full

Covering layer(s): First: Glass fibre 3B
                         Intermediate: Glass fibre 3B
                         Top: Glass fibre 3B
                         Bonding of covering layer(s): full

Applied finish: Chippings

Accessories: Edge trim

L23:   <u>PRODUCTS</u>

A210   BITUMEN FELT: to BS 747, as given in schedule of types of covering.

R210   EXPANDED POLYSTYRENE INSULATION: to BS 3837, pre-felted.
Grade: HD
Thickness: 50mm
Manufacturer and reference:
to be approved.

R610   FIBREBOARD: to BS 1142:Part 3, thickness 13mm.

X510   EDGE TRIM and preformed angles:
Material and finish: mill finish aluminium
Manufacturer and reference:
Metalon Ltd, 14 St James St, Cardiff, Type PQ.

Y110   PRIMERS/BONDING COMPOUNDS: type(s) recommended for the purpose by sheet covering manufacturer.

Y611   CHIPPINGS:
Type: hard limestone
Size: 9mm

<u>WORKMANSHIP</u>

<u>GENERALLY/PREPARATION</u>

1301   QUALITY OF WORK: handle, store and lay sheets and ancillary materials neatly to manufacturer's recommendations to make the whole sound and weathertight at the earliest opportunity before Practical Completion. Repair any defects as quickly as practicable to minimise damage and nuisance.

L23   <u>Felt sheet roof coverings</u> (continued)   L23

2071 SUITABILITY OF BASE: before laying coverings ensure that roof is to correct falls and all preliminary work including fixing of roof outlets to correct levels is complete. Base for sheeting must be clean and dry. Sub-contractor must confirm to Main Contractor and SO his agreement that the base is suitable.

2271 JOINTS IN BASE: cover with 150mm wide felt strip bonded at edges only.

2501 INSULATION: lay as specified, with staggered end joints and all joints close-butted.

2551 FIBREBOARD OVERLAY: fully bond to insulation by applying hot bonding compound to fibreboard and not to insulation. Lay with staggered, close-butted joints, to break joint with insulation.

2651 MOISTURE-ABSORBENT MATERIALS: lay sheets to cover dry-laid moisture-absorbent base or insulation on the same day as the base or insulation is laid. Seal exposed edges of base or insulation at the end of each day's work or at the first sign of rain.

   <u>LAYING SHEETS/ACCESSORIES/FINISHES</u>

3321 BITUMEN FELT: lay sheets in the direction of the roof slope with 50mm side and 75mm end laps, all fully sealed. Break bond between layers.

3321A DRESS FELT to eaves trim and seal to aluminium. Dress felt over timber fillet under roof tiles.

5101 VENTS:
   1. Position vents evenly over the roof area, one to every 4m².
   2. Do not prime or apply adhesive to base below vents.
   3. Prime skirt of vents before felting if recommended by manufacturer.

5451 BONDED CHIPPINGS FINISH:
   1. Apply as soon as the roof is clear of other sub-trades.
   2. Apply bitumen dressing compound and immediately dress with chippings closely bedded at the rate of 16kg/m².
   3. Remove loose chippings.

13 Specifications for specialist works

One of the contractual duties of the architect under the JCT Standard Form of Building Contract is to instruct the contractor as to the expenditure of Prime Cost and Provisional Sums. This he does by means of an architect's instruction or a Standard Form for nomination of subcontractors. However, beforehand he is generally required to obtain quotations for any work of a specialist nature or any special items of equipment selected for the works. These quotations are generally invited on special printed forms issued under the sanction of RIBA as follows:

Standard Form of Tender for Nominated Subcontractors for work involving both specialist labour and materials, that is, generally supply and fix items.
Form of Tender for use by Nominated Suppliers for the supply and delivery only of selected specified components or material.

Both of these forms, once properly completed with the relevant information, gives the potential subcontractor or supplier full details of the contractual arrangements envisaged for the works so that he is under no misapprehension of his duties and liabilities in this respect and can formulate his tender accordingly.

In addition to the conditions of contract, the tenderers will also need to be supplied with complete details of the specific requirements of the work or the components for which they are tendering. A short, specialist specification must therefore be prepared and attached to the complete inquiry document; this will then provide a full, complete and specific description of the architect's requirements.

Specifications for nominated sub-contractors

The standard form of tender for such specialist works is an all-embracing document suitable for a wide range of specialist works. These include:
Supply and erection of structural steelwork
Supply and erection of precast concrete frames and beams
Supply and fixing of masonry or precast concrete cladding
Supply and fixing of purpose made windows and doors
Supply and fixing of specialist flooring
Electrical intallations
Mechanical engineering installations
Sanitary pipework above ground, etc.

The document covers such contractual matters as:

Details of the job and the work involved
The name of the building owner, architect, quantity surveyor and consultant engineer
   (if applicable)
The name of the main contractor (if appointed)

It also gives all details of the conditions of tender applicable to a subcontractor, the location of the site, the type and location of the access and any order of works stipulated by the building owner. In addition, full details of attendance provided under the main contract by the contractor as described in the bills of quantities or the specification are incorporated in respect of:

Scaffolding, plant and hoisting
Temporary lighting and power
Materials (if any) to be provided by the main contractor
Unloading and distributing facilities
Additional facilities and services

Much of the specialized work carried out under nominated subcontracts is controlled by specific Codes of Practice and in all cases where these are applicable their directions should form the basis for the specialist specification. Most CP are 'deemed to satisfy' requirements of the Building Regulations, and divergence from them could cause problems and difficulties on site. A schedule of these codes in general use in building works is given under the separate trade headings in Chapter 6.

The following example has been prepared to show the general format applicable and to indicate how a short specification can be prepared for supply and installation. Of course, each separate inquiry would require a different content relating both to the basic material and the specific subcontract as well as to the relevant BS and Codes of Practice.

Example: Code of Practice Method

Project: New House and Garage
           Plot 2, The Avenue
           Hastleigh, Surrey

To: Biggs & Hill Ltd
           Plumbing and Heating Engineers
           23 Low Road, Mitcham, Surrey

Subcontract works: Supply and installation of single pipe stack, wastes and traps.

                                                        Ivor Brown, RIBA
November 1976   Chartered Architect

1   Specification and schedule of material and works.
    Supply, deliver to site and install complete 1 no. single pipe stack complete with all
    required bosses and junctions, horizontal wastes and traps as required in accordance
    with the drawing no. WD8/427 attached and the following specification. The conditions

of tendering are the enclosed Standard Form of Tender for Nominated Subcontractors which is to be completed and returned to the architect by the date indicated in the letter of invitation to tender accompanying this specification.

2   The materials to be used in the construction of the stack and ventilating shaft will be as follows:

Main stack, branch for WC to be cast iron to BS 416: 1973.
Alternatives may be incorporated (uPVC to BS 4514: 1983).
Pipes for basin and bath waste of copper to BS 2871, Pt 2: 1972 (uPVC to BS 5255: 1976).
Traps for basin and bath to be copper to BS 1184: 1976 (uPVC to BS 5255: 1976).
All necessary branches and bossed connections shall be provided.

3   The whole of the stack, wastes and traps will be designed, fabricated and fixed strictly in accordance with the relevant clauses of BS 5572: 1978. The stack will be jointed to the s.g.s. drain socket provided at ground floor level immediately below the stack with a flexible connection and an approved dome or grating fitted to the head of the ventilating shaft. The shaft will be set to pass through the roof, extending . . . mm above the roof slope to comply with the Building Regulations and provided with a Code 4 lead slate and tail soldered to the stack and neatly dressed between and over the plain roof tiles. (uPVC will require a drain connector at the foot and a Vari pitch pipe flashing to weather the roof penetration.)

4   The installation shall be tested to the satisfaction of the architect and the local authority and left perfect, air and watertight on completion.

Specifications for nominated suppliers

The standard form of tender for the supply and delivery of specified materials or components for fixing by the main contractor is also an all-embracing document suitable for a wide range of items. These include:

Doors, door sets and ironmongery
Supply only of standard windows
Sanitary fittings
Kitchen fittings and equipment
Gates and similar ironwork, etc.

This document, like that prepared for specialist subcontractors, covers such contractual matters as:

The names of building owner, architect and quantity surveyor (if applicable)
Details of the site, its location and access
Special requirements (if any) for delivery
Terms of payment and cash discounts
Returnable packings

General conditions as to supply, variation of quality, replacement of defective items and delivery

A short specification or schedule of specific requirements must be added to the inquiry providing a full and careful description of the materials and components required. These descriptions may be dealt with in two ways.

1   By inspection, selection and description by means of the individual manufacturers trade list nomenclature or designation. This is the usual method for individual projects for the occupation of commissioning clients and ensures that only those items selected and approved are supplied.

2   By individual description related to the appropriate British Standard type by specific quote. This is the usual method employed where cost is more important than either style or (perhaps) design and the principal requirement is for good quality utility rather than personal preference (see the list in Chapter 6).

It is always advisable, when specific components have been selected and specified, to incorporate a reference to the specific British Standard as, in most cases, these refer also to matters of manufacture, compatability with other components and items of a similar nature.

Alternative methods for the preparation of a specification for components to be supplied by a nominated supplier are given below. The methods shown for the supply and delivery of sanitary fittings apply equally to most other items covered by Prime Cost Sums, the wording being varied to suit the manufacturing requirements material, the particular article and the relevant British Standards. These latter documents must be consulted to ensure that the proper selection of component type or material is made.

Example: Selected component method

Project: New House and Garage
　　　　　Plot 2, The Avenue
　　　　　Hastleigh, Surrey

To:　　　Messrs Jones & Lack Ltd
　　　　　Builders Merchants
　　　　　4 High Street, Redhill, Surrey

Materials and goods: Sanitary fittings

　　　　　　　　　　　　　　　　　　　　　　　　Ivor Brown, RIBA
November 1976　　　　　　　　　　　　　　　Chartered Architect

1   Specification and schedule of materials
Supply and deliver to site sanitary fittings in accordance with this specification and schedule. The conditions of tendering are as incorporated in the attached Form of Tender for use by Nominated Suppliers which is to be completed and returned to the architect by the date indicated in the letter of invitation to tender accompanying this specification.

2   The sanitary fittings will be supplied strictly to the patterns and colours selected and described in the schedule and also comply, where applicable to the following:

Ceramic wash basins	BS 1188: 1974
Cast iron bath	BS 1189: 1972
WC pans	BS 5503, Pt 2: 1977
Flushing cisterns	BS 1125: 1973
Taps	BS 1010, Pt 2: 1973
Bath overflows and wastes for sanitary appliances	BS 3380: 1982
Ball valve	BS 1212: Pt 1: 1953; Pt 2: 1970; Pt 3: 1979
Plastic floats	BS 2456: 1973

3   The items shall be carefully packed and protected and delivered to site complete with all necessary fittings and fixings as provided by the manufacturer to meet the main contractor's installation programme.

4   Schedule of items
   1 no.   Thryfords 'Crescent' close coupled syphonic pattern vitreous china closet suite with valveless fittings, pottery syphon and bottom outlet with matching plastic seat and cover.
   1 no.   500 x 465 mm Thryfords 'Sola' vitreous china basin and pedestal with painted wall support complete with c.p. 'Starlite' basin taps and c.p. chain waste.
   1 no.   1700 x 750 x 545 mm Vogue 'Mayfair' porcelain enamelled cast iron bath with swept down front, integral soap and sponge rack fitted with c.p. handgrip and centre tap holes complete with c.p. 'Starlite' bath pillar taps, integral bath overflow, c.p. waste plug and chain, side and end panels.

   All items will be supplied to selected colour 'Pampas'.

Example: British Standard component method

Project: Extension to Mettaloy Ltd
         Bridge Street, Stockton

To: Jones & Lack Ltd
         Builders Merchants
         4 High Street, Redhill, Surrey

Materials and goods: Sanitary fittings

Ivor Brown, RIBA
Chartered Architect

November 1976

1   Specification and schedule of materials
   Supply and deliver to site sanitary fittings in accordance with this specification and sche-

dule. The conditions of tendering are as incorporated in the attached Form of Tender for use by Nominated Suppliers which is to be completed and returned to the architect by the date indicated in the letter of invitation to tender accompanying this specification.

2   The items shall be carefully packed and protected and delivered to site complete with all necessary fittings and fixings as provided by the manufacturer to meet the main contractor's installation programme.

3   <u>Schedule of items</u>

8 no.   white vitreous china WC pans with 'S' trap to BS 5503, Pt 2: 1977.

8 no.   9-litre white vitreous enamelled pressed steel cisterns complete with rubber cone connectors and uPVC flush pipes for low level installation to BS 1125: 1973.

8 no.   500 x 465 mm white vitreous china wash basins Type B to BS 1188: 1974 complete with pair white enamelled cast iron cantilever brackets, pair 12 mm c.p. screw down taps to BS 1010, Pt 2: 1973 and c.p. waste complete with plug and chain to BS 3380: 1982.

1 no.   4.8 m 8-stall stainless steel slab urinal complete with 7 no. integral divisions and 2 return ends and integral channel with single outlet at centre to BS 4880, Pt 1: 1972, complete with c.p. domed and hinged outlet grating, stainless steel flush and sparge pipe to BS 4127, Pt 2: 1972 with sufficient fixing clips and white vitreous enamelled pressed steel automatic flushing cistern complete with feeding device, syphon and cover to BS 1876: 1972.

14 Schedules of rates

A problem which occurs in all works carried out under a specification and drawings contract (where quantities do not form part of the contract) is the pricing of variations. Where a priced bill of quantities is available the computation of variations against similar items in the priced bill is a relatively simple matter; only dissimilar items requiring either a negotiated rate or a daywork account. Where the tender sum has been calculated on drawings and specifications and a lump sum offer made and accepted, some method for arriving at agreed values for extras or variations is essential.

While some contractors may be willing to open up their estimating papers in order to agree costs, this tends to happen only where a close and harmonious relationship has grown up between the builder and architect. For the majority of contracts, two methods for agreeing costs are in general use:

1 Requesting individual estimates from the builder for each and every variation to the original contract. This is a painstaking method of working and can lead to serious delays in the progress of the work. However, it does allow for each extra to be submitted to the employer for approval before the work is ordered or authorized. In the main this method is only applicable to very large or important variations or where specifically requested by the employer.

2 Ordering the work to be carried out under 'daywork' rates. In the appendix to the JCT Standard Form of Contract, percentages are inserted as follows for:

Labour
Material
Plant

The builder will have been requested in the Form of Tender to provide percentages for each of these three items, to cover in total his profit, overheads and all 'on costs' over and above the net value of any work carried out under daywork rates; these percentages are taken into account when considering the tenders.

In addition, while the cost of labour and plant are charged either according to national rates or subcontractor's hire charge invoices, the cost and value of materials can vary considerably depending on the business acumen of the buyer, the quantity and the quality of the material, and the distance it has to be transported to site. Consequently, to ensure a fair and reasonable price for the materials likely to be used in variations a schedule of rates of materials specified in the works should form part of the tender, the basic schedule being drawn up and forming part of the Form of Tender and priced by the estimator after he has prepared his estimate and entered his offer.

The schedule of rates, therefore, comprises a schedule of materials used in the work specified, against which the builder's estimator adds the unit monetary value of the material (per cubic metre, metre super, etc.) on which he has based the particular works in his estimate, for example:

Sharp sand/cubic metre
Cement/tonne
Facing bricks/thousand
etc.

These rates must be substantiated by presenting supplier's quotations. It is now possible to measure and price the majority of variations to the fabric on a measure and value basis against agreed percentages (to cover overheads, profit, etc.), on national wage rates set against time sheets for each operation and on an agreed value for materials. Care must be taken to have daywork sheets submitted in accordance with the terms of the contract as the work proceeds, and not in a thick wad at the end of the contract when all is covered up and forgotten.

In addition to using the schedule of rates for pricing variations, the items incorporated in it can be used under the Standard Form of Building Contract for fluctuations in material costs. The schedule should be so prepared and the contractor's attention drawn to this matter.

Example: Schedule of basic rates

Project . . . .

. . . .

Labour   Craftsmen   per hour

Labourers   per hour

Material   *Rate*   *Quantity*

Date of Tender: Contractor:

The rates provided in this schedule are for adjustment as provided in clauses 13 and 39 of the Standard Form of Building Contract; and clause 3.6 of the Agreement for Minor Building Works.

Appendix: Glossary of building and construction terms

There are a number of words in common use in specification writing which should be avoided as either unnecessary, superfluous or inaccurate. In most cases simple and more convenient words are readily available. Some unacceptable words are:

best quality — a term freely used but with no real significance.

etc. — a vague term, lacking specific direction, and to be avoided.

execute — an old-fashioned term which could be replaced by the phrase 'carry out', for example, 'The contractor shall carry out . . . .'

perform — similar to execute.

refix — to take from store and replace in position; this term generally refers to original, not new, material (also renew, replace).

A number of technical words occur regularly in building specifications, but often neither writers nor site staff understands their correct meaning. A selection of these terms is given below. (See also BS 3589: 1963 Glossary of General Building Terms, and BS 4949: 1973: Glossary of terms relating to building performance, and the glossaries incorporated in Chapter 6.)

apron — a vertical or horizontal flashing surrounding a projection, e.g. chimney stack.

batten — a scantling of wood not exceeding 100 x 25.

bead — a small convex moulding, usually run on a small wood section used to retain a panel or pane of glass.

bond — an arrangement of units forming a wall to ensure stability; the adhesion between two materials or surfaces.

bonder — a structural member of brick or stone extending through the full thickness of the structural wall.

bracket — a horizontal projection to carry a load.

carcassing — the formation of the main structure of a building (also mechanical services).

carcassing timbers — timbers employed in a structural function.

casing — a covering to protect (e.g. steel or pipes).

casings — jamb linings or framing.

coping — a protective covering to the top of a wall.

corbel — a cantilevered bracket usually of brick or stone.

cradling — supports surrounding steel to receive a casing (usually of timber).

damp-proof course — a material placed within a wall or chimney stack to resist the passage of water.
damp-proof membrane — a damp-proof course incorporated within a floor.
decking — prefabricated units used for the construction of a roof or floor.
dumpling — unexcavated ground surrounded by a trench or excavation.

fascia — a horizontal facing to eaves or cornice.
finishings — treatment or fixtures to internal surfaces to convert the carcass to a complete building (excluding services).
fitting — a secondary element attached to rather than built into a structure.
fixture — a secondary element built into rather than attached to a structure.
flashing — a strip of impermeable material provided to protect a joint from water penetration.
formwork — temporary moulds to enclose and support wet concrete.

ground — timber fixing pieces plugged to a wall (e.g. for skirtings).

Insitu — materials or components assembled or cast in their permanent situation.

joinery — timber and timber products prepared and assembled into components, fittings and finishings.
joist — a beam, usually of timber, forming one of a number of parts of a floor, ceiling or flat roof.

kerb — a low upstand.

lintel — a beam spanning an opening.

made ground — ground built up from waste or excavated material.
monolithic — a continuous undivided mass.

padstone — a block of concrete built into a wall to distribute the load from a beam.
pier — a column of brick, block or stones.
pilaster — a projection from a wall, either decorative or load-bearing.
planking and strutting — the timber supports provided to the sides of an excavation to withstand the lateral thrust of the soil.
plinth — an architectural feature forming the lowest part of a wall or column and usually projecting beyond the wall face.
precast — cast and lifted into position (as opposed to *in situ*).
pugging — a layer of material placed between structural members to provide insulation.
purlin — a horizontal member supported on struts or trusses and providing intermediate support to inclined roof rafters.

rafter — an inclined beam, one of a series providing support to pitched roofing.

raker — an inclined beam.

rebate — a longitudinal groove or channel.

scantling — a section of timber usually quartered.

services — generally the fabrication and installation of water, gas, heating and electricity (does not apply to mechanical equipment, e.g. lifts).

shore — a temporary support to a building (also needle, prop and strut).

sidings — a covering to an external wall or frame (e.g. weatherboarding).

sill — the base of an opening, usually designed to throw stormwater clear of the wall below.

soffit — the underside of a structural member.

spreader — a structural member inserted in a wall to spread a load.

templet — a pattern used for setting out (especially in masonry).

trim — the finishings provided around an opening.

weathering — an inclined upper surface to assist in shedding water (e.g. to copings and sills).

   — sunk weathering where the bottom of a rebate is weathered (e.g. in sills and upper surfaces of projecting cornices.

Index